LUNCHBOX SALADS

Naomi Twigden and Anna Pinder

Da Capo

LIFE
LONG

INTRODUCTION

HEY

We're two cooks who love all food and enjoy eating healthily for the way it makes us feel.

After training and working as chefs and in the food industry in London and abroad, a few years ago we decided to start a food delivery business in London called Lunch BXD. We felt that so much "healthy" food was restrictive or dull and we wanted to show how it could be zingy, filling and flavorful, and naturally healthy too. Each morning we prepared lunchboxes and then hopped on our bicycles to deliver them to offices around the city. It was a whirlwind adventure of quinoa, kale and our signature satay sauce.

This book contains everything we learned along the way about making fast, fresh and simple good food. We want to show you that salad can be much more than just lettuce leaves.

Hope you enjoy.

Naomi Twigden and Anna Pinder
@bxdideas

HOW THIS BOOK WORKS

The aim of this book is to offer easy, approachable, affordable, convenient, substantial AND vibrant salad inspiration for every working day. All the recipes here use 10 or fewer easy-to-buy ingredients and take no more than 30 minutes to make.

Our salads are substantial portions designed to keep your energy levels up throughout the afternoon. Every recipe makes 2 portions and everything will keep well for 2 days in the fridge. (We've included specific packing instructions with each recipe to avoid soggy leaves at lunchtime.)

We sometimes suggest packing the dressing separately. To do this, line a mug or glass with 2 pieces of plastic wrap. Make sure you have a good bit extra hanging over the sides of the mug/glass on all sides, then pour in the dressing or dip. Gather the extra plastic wrap and twist into a knot to seal the dressing inside. Pop the pouch into your lunchbox or bag. When you are ready to serve, pierce the plastic wrap with a fork or knife and pour the dressing out.

The recipes are designed to be cost-effective and repeat ingredients in different ways so you don't end up with lots of waste or a pantry full of different spices and grains. There's a suggested list of essential dry ingredients on page 7, which are used throughout this book. There is also an index on page 158, listing where every ingredient is used to help you make the best of any leftovers.

> "
> WE WANT TO SHOW YOU
> THAT SALAD CAN BE
> MUCH MORE THAN JUST
> LETTUCE LEAVES
> "

This is not a vegetarian cookbook but each chapter in this book is focused around a hero vegetable. They are our heroes because they are either the largest element of the dish or the star in terms of flavor. You'll find meat and fish ideas here too but we want to celebrate the versatility of veg, and break the misconception that you need meat and fish to make a meal.

Using vegetables over meat and fish cuts down costs—if you're making packed lunches you're probably aiming to save money, so by focusing on vegetables that's a lot easier to do.

By focusing on one main vegetable it is easier to find a recipe that uses up what is available and limits food waste too.

There's a lot in the press about why eating less meat is good for our health and the environment. We personally feel better on a balanced, colorful diet packed full of fresh vegetables.

Our recipes are easy to customize, though, to suit your taste buds or dietary preferences. Feel free to add chicken or swap cheese for tofu.

The recipes are your basic guide but cooking them should be creative and fun, so we've added tips throughout the book to help you get creative in the kitchen and use up what you have in the fridge or what is in season.

PANTRY ESSENTIALS

All our recipes have 10 ingredients or fewer and assume you already own oil, salt and pepper. To help keep costs down and minimize waste, the following ingredients would be handy to have in stock as they appear frequently throughout the book.

CANNED/JARRED
Chickpeas
Sweet corn kernels
Tuna
Kidney beans
Butter beans
Jarred roasted red peppers

SAUCES
Cider vinegar (or balsamic or white wine)
Soy sauce
Peanut butter (preferably sugar-free)
Honey or brown sugar
Harissa
Tahini

DRY STORE
Unsalted cashews
Sliced almonds
Pumpkin seeds
Sesame seeds
Unsweetened shredded coconut

GRAINS
Brown rice/wild rice
Green lentils
Whole wheat pasta
Quinoa
Dry noodles

SPICES
Ground cumin
Crushed red pepper flakes
Ground cinnamon
Smoked paprika
Dried Italian herbs
Curry powder

FRESH/FROZEN
Lemons/limes
Garlic
Ginger
Frozen peas
Frozen shelled edamame beans
Greek yogurt

We specify different nuts, seeds and pasta types in our recipes for variety and flavor but all types would work well.

UTENSILS
All recipes are easy to make with basic cooking equipment. A blender is required for some recipes as is a spiralizer. If you don't have a spiralizer, vegetables can often be bought pre-spiralized or you can shave them into ribbons with a peeler instead.

OILS
We recommend different oils based on the flavor or how they work at high temperatures but they are mostly interchangeable—in general we use mild olive oil for drizzling and dressing and vegetable oil or coconut oil for cooking.

SQUASH

SQUASH NOODLES WITH SHRIMP
+ COCONUT-LIME DRESSING

INGREDIENTS:

1 cup frozen shelled edamame beans
½ large butternut squash (the thinner
 part with no seeds)
coconut oil
2 handfuls of raw peeled shrimp
2 red peppers
2 portions of Coconut-lime Dressing
 (see page 153)

TRY THIS…

Swap the coconut dressing for another, such
as one of our pestos/Satay Dressing/Peanut
Teriyaki Sauce *(see pages 154–156)*.

METHOD:

Put the edamame in a bowl of cold water and
set aside to thaw.

Peel the squash and spiralize into noodles
(or grate/shave with a peeler). Place in a frying
pan with 2 teaspoons of coconut oil and fry over
medium-high heat for 4–5 minutes until just
cooked through and slightly crisp. Keep stirring.
Remove the squash from the pan with a slotted
spoon and set aside in a bowl.

Add the shrimp to the same pan with a little
more coconut oil and fry over medium-high heat
for 4–5 minutes until pink and opaque. Add to
the squash and allow to cool.

Meanwhile, remove the core and seeds from the
red peppers, then cut into thin strips. Drain the
edamame. Add the peppers and edamame to
the squash and shrimp and toss together. Season
with salt and pepper.

To pack: Spoon the salad into two lunchboxes.
Pack the dressing separately.

ROAST DUKKAH SQUASH + KALE
WITH RICOTTA

INGREDIENTS:

1 butternut squash
olive oil
2½ cups chopped kale
20 fresh mint/cilantro leaves
lime juice
⅓ cup ricotta (or crumbled feta)

Dukkah
1 teaspoon ground coriander and/or cumin
1 handful of sesame seeds
1 handful of mixed nuts (sliced almonds/
  pistachios/hazelnuts work well, or a
  combination)

TRY THIS…

· Add a 15-oz. can of corn or chickpeas, drained
  and rinsed.

· Try the dukkah on poached eggs and avocado
  at breakfast.

METHOD:

Preheat the oven to 350°F and bring a large pot
of water to a boil. Peel the squash and cut into
large chunks, discarding the seeds. Once the
water reaches a boil, add the squash with a pinch
of salt. Boil for 5 minutes until just soft.

Drain and place on a baking sheet with a little
oil and seasoning. Roast for 15–20 minutes until
golden brown and slightly crisp. Turn the chunks
every few minutes.

While the squash is being prepared, boil another
2 cups of water. Place the chopped kale in a
bowl, cover with boiled water and add a pinch
of salt. Leave for 5 minutes, then drain and rinse
under cold water.

Toast the dukkah spices in a dry frying pan over
medium heat, stirring all the time, for 1 minute
until fragrant. Add the sesame seeds and nuts,
and stir until browned. Blitz in a food processor,
or pound using a mortar and pestle, until
roughly ground.

Add the kale to the squash and stir in the dukkah
along with the torn mint or cilantro leaves, a little
olive oil, lime juice to taste and salt and pepper.

To pack: Spoon the salad into two lunchboxes and
dot the ricotta on top.

TIP: Dukkah is an Egyptian spice blend. Make a bigger batch—it will keep for weeks stored in
an airtight container—because it makes a great crunchy topper for any simple salad.

ROAST ROOT VEGETABLES WITH AVOCADO, FETA + PEA DIP

INGREDIENTS:

1 small butternut squash
2 red onions
2 carrots
coconut/olive oil
1½ cups baby spinach leaves

Dip
2 handfuls of frozen peas
1 avocado
¼ cup crumbled feta
15 fresh mint leaves
lemon juice

TRY THIS…

· Swap the peas for a handful of frozen shelled edamame beans, thawed in a bowl of cold water for 1–2 minutes, or canned butter beans, drained and rinsed.

· Bake a chicken breast with the vegetables for the final 18–20 minutes. Shred the chicken, using two forks to pull the meat apart.

· Make extra dip and serve on toast at breakfast with tomatoes and crisp-fried chorizo.

METHOD:

Preheat the oven to 400°F and bring a large pot of water to a boil. Peel the squash, red onions and carrots and cut into 1-inch chunks, discarding the squash seeds.

Add the squash to the pot with a pinch of salt. Simmer for 2 minutes. Add the carrots and onion and simmer for another 2 minutes. Drain the vegetables and spread out on a baking sheet. Drizzle with a little oil, salt, and pepper. Mix together. Roast for 25 minutes until cooked through and crisp. Stir every few minutes. Cool.

While the vegetables are roasting, thaw the peas in a bowl of cold water for 1–2 minutes; drain. Scoop the flesh from the avocado into a food processor and add the feta, mint and peas. Blitz briefly (it should be chunky). Season, adding lemon juice to taste and as much water/oil as you need to loosen to a dip-like consistency.

To pack: Once the roasted vegetables are cool, toss with the spinach, then spoon into two lunchboxes. Pack the dip separately.

CRUNCHY SQUASH SATAY SALAD

INGREDIENTS:

1 small butternut squash
coconut/olive oil
¾ cup quinoa
½ red cabbage
1 green pepper
2 portions of Satay Dressing *(see page 156)*

TRY THIS…

· Drizzle oil and honey over a chicken breast
and sprinkle with some sesame seeds. Bake in
a 400°F oven for 18–20 minutes. Slice and add
to the lunchboxes.

· Sprinkle with toasted and lightly crushed
peanuts for extra crunch.

METHOD:

Preheat the oven to 400°F and bring 1½ cups
of water to a boil in a small saucepan. Peel the
squash and cut into roughly 1-inch chunks,
discarding the seeds. Place on a baking sheet
with a splash of oil and a pinch of salt. Roast for
15–20 minutes until tender and golden. Halfway
through cooking, give the tray a shake/stir to
prevent the squash chunks from sticking.

Meanwhile, add the quinoa to the saucepan of
boiling water. Cover, reduce heat to low and
simmer for 15–20 minutes until al dente. Fluff
with a fork.

While the quinoa cooks, remove the outer leaves
and core from the red cabbage, then thinly slice.
Dice the pepper into small strips, discarding the
core and seeds.

Mix the cabbage and pepper into the quinoa and
season with a pinch of salt. Toss the squash with
the satay dressing.

To pack: Spread the quinoa in two lunchboxes
and pile the squash on top.

JERK CHICKEN + SQUASH
WITH QUINOA + PEAS

INGREDIENTS:

1 small butternut squash
2 skinless boneless chicken breasts
⅔ cup quinoa
¾ cup frozen peas
2 tablespoons finely chopped fresh cilantro
juice of 2 limes

Jerk rub
1½ tablespoons sugar/honey
1½ tablespoons coconut oil
2 tablespoons store-bought jerk seasoning
    (or 2 teaspoons ground allspice, 1½ teaspoons
    dried thyme/mixed Italian herbs and a good
    pinch of ground cinnamon)

TRY THIS…

· Replace the chicken or quinoa with a 15.5-oz.
  can of black beans, drained and rinsed/
  2 handfuls of chopped kale, blanched in boiling
  water for 5 minutes/1 chopped mango.

· Add a sprinkle of dried shredded coconut to
  the chicken and squash for the final 5 minutes
  of cooking, for extra sweetness.

· Use the same rub on chicken thighs or
  drumsticks on a barbecue.

· Replace the jerk rub with Peanut Teriyaki
  Sauce *(see page 156)*.

METHOD:

Preheat the oven to 400°F and bring a large pot
of water to a boil. Peel the squash and chop into
1-inch cubes. Add to the pot of boiling water with
pinch of salt and cook for 5 minutes. Drain and
spread out on a baking sheet with the chicken.

Mix all the jerk rub ingredients together with some
seasoning and use to thoroughly coat the squash
and chicken. Bake for 18–20 minutes until the
chicken is cooked through. Stir every 5 minutes.

Meanwhile, boil 1⅓ cup of water in a small
saucepan. Add the quinoa and a pinch of salt.
Cover, reduce heat and simmer for 15–20 minutes
until tender. Fluff with a fork. Thaw the peas in a
bowl of cold water for 1–2 minutes; drain.

Cut the cooked chicken at an angle into thin
slices. Mix together the quinoa, chicken, squash,
peas, cilantro and any juices from the baking
sheet. Season and add lime juice to taste.

To pack: Spoon into two lunchboxes.

MOROCCAN SQUASH, GREEN BEANS, APRICOTS + PISTACHIOS

INGREDIENTS:

1 red onion
1 small piece fresh ginger
coconut/olive oil
2 tablespoons ras el hanout (or 1½ teaspoons
   ground cinnamon, 2 teaspoons ground cumin
   and 1½ teaspoons ground coriander)
2 tablespoons tomato purée
1 small butternut squash
6 oz. green beans
8 fresh (or dried) apricots
⅓ cup unsalted pistachios (or sliced almonds)

TRY THIS...

· Garnish with fresh cilantro and a drizzle of
  honey.

· Add sliced chicken to the softened spiced onion
  and fry together until cooked through before
  adding the rest of the ingredients.

· Create a tagine: add a 14.5-oz. can of diced
  tomatoes and a 15.5-oz. can of chickpeas,
  rinsed and drained, after the final 2 minutes
  of cooking. Simmer for 10–15 minutes until
  thickened.

· Create a lamb tagine: add 6–8 oz. ground lamb
  to the softened spiced onion and brown well
  before adding the squash, beans and apricots,
  followed by the tomatoes and chickpeas
  (as above).

METHOD:

Boil a large pot of water. Peel and finely dice the
onion and ginger. Place in a pan with a little oil,
all the other spices and the tomato purée. Fry
over low heat for about 8 minutes until the onion
is soft, stirring occasionally.

Meanwhile, peel the squash and chop into 1-inch
pieces, discarding the seeds. Add to the pot of
boiling water with a pinch of salt. Cook for 6–7
minutes. Drain and rinse under cold water.

Trim the green beans and cut in half. Place in
a pan with a pinch of salt and cover with water;
bring to a boil. Cook for 3–5 minutes until just
tender but still very crunchy. Drain and rinse
under cold water.

Cut the apricots into quarters, discarding the
stones. (If using dried apricots, pour boiled water
over them and leave for 5 minutes to plump up
before draining and roughly dicing.)

Add the squash, beans and apricots to the onions
and cook everything together for 2 minutes.
Keep stirring. Season with salt and pepper to
taste.

Toast the nuts over medium heat for 1–2 minutes
in a dry pan.

To pack: Allow the squash salad to cool before
spooning into two lunchboxes. Sprinkle the
nuts on top.

SAGE + SQUASH PASTA WITH PROSCIUTTO, ARUGULA + LEMON

INGREDIENTS:

1 cup whole wheat fusilli
coconut/olive oil
1 small butternut squash
8 fresh sage leaves
²/₃ cup frozen peas
½ lemon
2½ cups arugula
2 oz. Parmesan
4 slices prosciutto

TRY THIS…

· Swap the prosciutto and Parmesan for
cooked bacon and Cheddar.

· Stir in a tablespoon of crème fraîche for
a creamier sauce.

· Add crushed red pepper flakes or a minced hot
pepper for heat.

· Sprinkle a handful of toasted pine nuts
over the arugula.

METHOD:

Boil a large pot of water. Add the pasta with
a large pinch of salt and cook according to
package directions until al dente. Drain the
pasta, keeping back half a ladle of pasta water to
add to the sauce at the end. Mix the pasta with a
little oil to prevent sticking.

While the pasta is cooking, peel the squash and
chop into 1-inch cubes, discarding the seeds.
Place in another pan, cover with water and bring
to a boil; cook for 5 minutes until just tender.
Drain.

Tip the squash into a frying pan and tear the
sage leaves over the top. Add a little oil and fry
over a medium heat for 5 minutes until golden
brown all over. Meanwhile, thaw the peas in a
bowl of cold water for 1–2 minutes; drain.

Stir the pasta, reserved pasta water and peas
into the squash. Mix well. Zest in the lemon and
season with juice to taste and a good amount of
black pepper.

To pack: Allow to cool, then spoon into two
lunchboxes and pile the arugula on top. Grate
over the Parmesan and top with the roughly
torn prosciutto.

TIP: Adding some of the pasta cooking liquid at the end helps thicken the sauce
as the liquid contains starch from the pasta.

SQUASH NOODLES WITH PESTO-BAKED CHICKEN

INGREDIENTS:

2 skinless boneless chicken breasts
2 portions of Green Pesto *(see page 154)*
1 small butternut squash
coconut/olive oil
²/₃ cup frozen peas
1 x 8.5 oz. can sweet corn kernels

METHOD:

Preheat the oven to 400°F. Place the chicken on a baking sheet. Coat with half the pesto, then bake for 18–20 minutes until cooked through. Cool, then slice at an angle.

While the chicken is in the oven, peel the squash and remove the seeds. Spiralize the bottom, thinner part of the squash (the seeded half won't spiralize) and shave the seeded part into ribbons with a peeler. (If you don't have a spiralizer you can shave the whole squash into ribbons.) Place the squash in a frying pan with a little oil and seasoning. Fry over high heat for 3–5 minutes until just cooked.

Thaw the peas in a bowl of cold water for 1–2 minutes; drain. Drain the corn.

To pack: Spoon the peas, corn and noodles into the lunchboxes. Place the chicken on top and add the remaining pesto.

TRY THIS...

Swap the chicken for 2 smoked trout fillets.

TIP:

Having frozen peas on hand makes it easy to bulk out meals with an extra portion of vegetables. If thawed quickly in a bowl of cold water (they don't need cooking), they will keep more of their crunch and color.

SQUASH, CASHEW + SPINACH SALAD WITH TAHINI DRESSING

INGREDIENTS:

1 red onion
coconut/olive oil
1 small butternut squash
½ cup unsalted cashews
2 handfuls of pomegranate seeds
1½ cups baby spinach leaves

Dressing
2 teaspoons tahini
2 tablespoons natural yogurt
1 teaspoon vegetable oil
1 teaspoon honey
lemon juice

TRY THIS…

Swap the tahini dressing and pomegranate seeds for one of our pestos *(see pages 154–155)* and feta.

METHOD:

Peel and dice the onion. Fry in a pan with a little oil over a low heat for about 10 minutes until soft.

Meanwhile, peel the squash and chop into 1-inch chunks, discarding the seeds. Place in a pan with a pinch of salt and cover with water; bring to a boil. Cook for 5 minutes until just soft. Drain.

Add the squash and a little more oil to the onion. Turn up the heat and fry for 2–3 minutes until slightly golden. Remove the onion and squash and cool.

Wipe the pan dry. Lightly crush the nuts, then toast over medium heat in the dry pan for 2 minutes until golden brown.

Whisk the dressing ingredients together with 1 teaspoon water and season to taste with salt and pepper.

To pack: Mix the squash and onion with the nuts and spoon into two lunchboxes. Top with the pomegranate seeds and spinach. Pack the dressing separately.

SWEET
POTATO

4 IDEAS FOR
BAKED SWEET POTATOES

INGREDIENTS:

2 sweet potatoes
coconut/olive oil
1½ cups baby spinach leaves
plus one of the topping options
(see opposite and overleaf)

METHOD:

Preheat the oven to 410°F and bring a large
pot of water to a boil. Cut the unpeeled sweet
potatoes lengthways in half and place in the pot
of boiling water with a pinch of salt. Boil for 6–8
minutes until just cooked through. (Test with a
knife in the center.) Drain.

Lay the sweet potato halves skin side down on
a baking sheet. Drizzle over a little oil and
season with salt and pepper. Bake for 20 minutes
until slightly crisp. While they are in the oven,
prepare one of the toppings. (Note that some of
the topping elements are baked with the sweet
potatoes.)

To pack: Cool the sweet potatoes (and the topping,
if necessary) before packing. Place the sweet
potato halves side by side in the lunchboxes and
spoon the topping alongside. Pile the spinach on
top or to the side.

Spring onion, prosciutto and chive topping

3 spring onions or scallions (white bulbs and
    most of the green)
4 slices prosciutto
3 tablespoons crème fraîche/natural yogurt
1 tablespoon finely snipped fresh chives

Finely slice the spring onions and prosciutto.

Once the sweet potatoes have been baking for
15 minutes, remove from the oven and scoop out
the flesh into a bowl (leave enough on the skin to
keep the shape). Mix with the topping ingredients,
season, then spoon back into the potato skins.

Return to the oven and bake for another 5 minutes.

Apple, beet and pecan slaw topping (above)

¹/₂ cup pecans
2 apples
3 cooked and peeled beets
15 fresh mint leaves
2 tablespoons crème fraîche/natural yogurt

Roughly chop the pecans and add to the
baking sheet with the sweet potatoes for the final
3 minutes of their cooking, to toast the nuts.

Grate the apples and beets into a sieve set over
the sink. Use your hands to squeeze out any
excess liquid. Tip into a bowl and fold in the torn
mint leaves. Mix in the crème fraîche. Stir the
toasted pecans through the slaw.

Smoky baked beans topping

1 small white/red onion
1 garlic clove
1 teaspoon smoked paprika
½ teaspoon ground cumin
olive oil
½ x 14.5-oz. can diced tomatoes
1½ oz. Cheddar
Worcestershire sauce (optional)
1 x 15.5-oz. can kidney beans
Tabasco (optional)

Peel and finely chop the onion. Peel and crush
the garlic. Fry together in a medium pan with
the spices and a splash of oil over low heat for
10 minutes until very soft. Add the tomatoes and
stir, then leave to simmer over medium heat for
8–10 minutes to reduce by half.

About 5 minutes before the sweet potatoes have
finished baking, grate the Cheddar over the top
of them and sprinkle with Worcestershire sauce,
if using.

Drain and rinse the beans. Stir into the tomato
sauce and season (add a little Tabasco, if you like).
Heat until piping hot.

Chili pepper and sesame tuna topping

2 tablespoons sesame seeds
2 x 5-oz. cans tuna in olive oil
1 fresh red/green chili pepper
2 spring onions or scallions (white bulbs and most
   of the green)
1 tablespoon finely chopped fresh cilantro
2 tablespoons soy sauce
1 teaspoon toasted sesame oil
1 lime

Sprinkle the sesame seeds over the sweet potatoes
while they are baking.

Drain and flake the tuna. Remove the seeds from
the chili pepper, then finely chop (use less than
the whole pepper if you've picked a particularly
hot variety). Thinly slice the spring onions on an
angle. Combine these prepared ingredients in a
bowl with the cilantro, soy sauce and sesame oil.
Zest the lime into the bowl and add the juice too.
Mix everything well.

SWEET POTATO + SPINACH NIÇOISE SALAD

INGREDIENTS:

2 sweet potatoes
3 tablespoons olive oil, plus extra for drizzling
2 salmon fillets, 4–6 oz. each
sea salt
lemon juice
2 eggs
10 cherry tomatoes
2 tablespoons whole grain mustard
¼ cup pumpkin seeds
1¾ cups baby spinach leaves

TRY THIS…

· Replace the salmon with canned tuna. Drain and roughly flake the tuna, then mix with a dollop of Greek yogurt, 1 tablespoon finely chopped fresh parsley, a squeeze of lemon juice and salt and pepper.

· Swap pumpkin seeds for mixed seeds or olives.

METHOD:

Preheat the oven to 400°F. Peel the sweet potatoes and cut into chunky, irregular-sized pieces. Place in a pan with a pinch of salt, cover with water and bring to a boil. Simmer for 3 minutes.

Drain and place on a baking sheet with a splash of oil and another pinch of salt. Bake for about 20 minutes until golden. Shake the tray every few minutes so the sweet potatoes don't stick.

While the sweet potatoes are in the oven, place the salmon on another baking sheet lined with foil, drizzle over a little oil and season with a pinch of sea salt and a squeeze of lemon. Bake for 12 minutes.

Meanwhile, put the eggs in a pan and cover with cold water by 1 inch. Bring to a boil over medium-high heat, then cover, remove from heat and set aside 8–10 minutes to hard boil. Drain and place in a bowl of cold water to cool quickly, then peel and cut in half.

Cut the cherry tomatoes half. Whisk the mustard with the 3 tablespoons oil, a squeeze of lemon juice and salt to taste.

To pack: Allow the sweet potatoes and salmon to cool. Arrange the sweet potatoes, salmon (whole or flaked), eggs and tomato halves in the lunchboxes and top with the pumpkin seeds and spinach. Pack the mustard dressing separately.

SWEET POTATO + RED LENTIL CAKES WITH A RAW SHREDDED SALAD

INGREDIENTS:

½ cup red lentils
2 sweet potatoes
2 teaspoons ground cumin
4 tablespoons snipped fresh chives
2 tablespoons sesame seeds
½ white cabbage
juice of 2 lemons
2½ cups arugula

METHOD:

Preheat the oven to 400°F. Put the lentils in a pot with 1½ cups water. Bring to a boil, then reduce heat to medium-low and simmer about 15 minutes until tender. Tip into a bowl and add a pinch of salt.

While the lentils are cooking, peel the sweet potatoes and chop roughly into small pieces, then place in a pan with a pinch of salt. Cover with water, bring to a boil and cook until just tender, about 10–15 minutes. Drain and return to the pan. Using a potato masher, gently crush the potatoes. Add to the bowl with the lentils.

Season the mashed sweet potato and lentils with the cumin, half of the chives and a pinch of salt. Mix well. Shape into 6 cakes. Coat the top and bottom of each cake with sesame seeds and place on a lined baking sheet. Bake for 10–12 minutes until golden. Flip over halfway through cooking.

Meanwhile, prepare the salad. Remove the outer leaves and stalk from the cabbage, then finely slice. Place in a bowl and toss with the lemon juice, remaining chives and a pinch of salt.

To pack: Allow the cakes to cool before packing. Place the cabbage salad on one side in the lunchboxes and the arugula on the other side. Arrange the cakes in the middle.

TRY THIS…

Add a heaping tablespoon of crumbled feta to the mashed sweet potato mix before forming it into cakes.

SWEET POTATO NACHOS

INGREDIENTS:

2 sweet potatoes
olive oil
2 tablespoons smoked paprika
1 red pepper
1 x 15.5-oz. can kidney beans
1 x 15.5-oz. can chickpeas
2 avocados
juice of ½ lemon
1 tablespoon finely chopped fresh cilantro

METHOD:

Preheat the oven to 400°F. Scrub the sweet potatoes and pat dry, then slice into thin rounds. Pile on a baking sheet. Drizzle over a little oil and season with salt and the smoked paprika. Toss together until evenly coated, then spread out in one layer. Bake for 15–20 minutes until golden brown on both sides. Turn over midway through cooking. Cool.

While the sweet potatoes are baking, remove the core and seeds from the red pepper, then cut into strips. Drain and rinse the kidney beans and chickpeas. Place these prepared ingredients in a bowl and season with salt and pepper.

Peel, pit and dice the avocados and toss with the lemon juice and cilantro. Season this guacamole.

To pack: Place the cooled sweet potato nachos on one side in the lunchboxes and the guacamole on the other side, with the bean salad in the middle.

TRY THIS...

· Turn this into Huevos Rancheros. Add cherry tomatoes, cut in half, and fry with the red pepper, beans and chickpeas in a splash of oil in an ovenproof frying pan for 10 minutes. Arrange the cooked sweet potato nachos over the surface and crack 2 eggs on top. Bake in a 350°F oven for 8–10 minutes until the eggs are cooked through. Serve warm with the guacamole or a dollop of sour cream.

· Pulled chicken is a great addition to the lunchboxes. Place 2 skinless boneless chicken breasts on a baking sheet. Drizzle over a little oil and season with a pinch of sea salt. Bake in a 400°F oven for 18–20 minutes until cooked through. Cool slightly, then pull the chicken apart using two forks. Toast a tablespoon of smoked paprika or ground cumin in a dry pan for 2 minutes and stir through the pulled chicken with a little more oil, salt and pepper.

TIP: If you have leftover avocado, freeze it (without the stone). Add it frozen to a breakfast smoothie.

TUNA STEAK + SWEET POTATO NOODLES WITH A SATAY SAUCE

INGREDIENTS:

METHOD:

2 large sweet potatoes
coconut/olive oil
7 oz. sugarsnap peas
¼ cup unsalted peanuts
2 fresh tuna steaks, 4–6 oz. each
2½ cups arugula
2 portions of Satay Dressing *(see page 156)*

Bring a small pot of water to a boil. Peel the sweet potatoes and spiralize. Place in a pan with a splash of oil and cook over medium-high heat, tossing gently with tongs, for 5–7 minutes until cooked through. Take care not to break up the noodles. Season and cool.

Place the sugarsnap peas in a bowl, cover with boiling water and leave for 3 minutes. Drain and rinse under cold water to stop the cooking.

While the sweet potatoes and sugarsnaps are being cooked, crush the peanuts and toast for 1–2 minutes over medium heat in a dry pan. Remove from the pan.

Turn the heat under the pan up to medium-high. Rub both sides of each tuna steak with oil and season with a pinch of sea salt. Place in the hot pan and sear for 1–2 minutes on each side. Remove from the pan and cool.

To pack: Pile the sweet potato noodles in one half of the lunchboxes. In the other half place the sugarsnap peas and arugula next to one another. Lay the cooked tuna steak on top of the noodles. When ready to serve, pour the dressing over all and sprinkle with the crushed, toasted peanuts.

TRY THIS…

Swap the tuna for salmon/peeled shrimp. If using salmon fillets, add a splash of oil and pinch of salt, then bake in a 400°F oven for 12 minutes. For raw shrimp, heat a pan with a splash of oil and cook the shrimp for about 4 minutes until pink, stirring frequently.

SWEET POTATO MISO + CHORIZO HASH

INGREDIENTS:

3 sweet potatoes
3 oz. chorizo
coconut/olive oil
4 oz. green beans
4 oz. broccolini
1½ cups chopped kale
4 teaspoons miso paste
2 tablespoons honey
2 teaspoons ginger paste

METHOD:

Scrub the sweet potatoes and chop into 1-inch pieces. Place in a pan, cover with water and add a pinch of salt. Bring to a boil and cook for 3–4 minutes until just soft. Drain and set to one side.

Slice the chorizo into rounds about ½ inch thick. Place the chorizo and cooked sweet potato in a frying pan with a splash of oil and fry for 2 minutes on each side until crisp. Remove and set aside (don't wash the pan).

Trim the green beans. Cut the green beans in half and the broccolini into shorter lengths if they are large. Place in a pan with the kale. Cover with water, add a pinch of salt and bring to a boil, then simmer over a medium heat for 4–5 minutes until just tender. Drain and rinse under cold water to stop the cooking.

Make the dressing by mixing together the miso, honey and ginger paste in the frying pan, adding a splash of hot water if needed to loosen (the dressing should be thick in consistency). Return the cooked sweet potato and chorizo to the pan and toss over medium-low heat until the sauce thickens to a glaze and coats the sweet potato. Lightly crush the potato with the back of a fork.

To pack: Once cool, gently toss all the ingredients together, then spoon into the lunchboxes.

TRY THIS…

Scatter crumbled feta/sesame seeds/crushed red pepper over the hash in the lunchbox.

CARROT, KALE + CHICKPEA SALAD WITH HONEY DRESSING + FETA

INGREDIENTS:

1 x 15.5-oz. can chickpeas
coconut/olive oil
4 carrots
2 teaspoons cumin/fennel seeds
   (or ground is fine)
2 cups chopped kale
1 tablespoon finely chopped fresh parsley
3 oz. feta

Dressing
1½ tablespoons honey
1 tablespoon olive oil
2 teaspoon cider vinegar

TRY THIS...

Stir some chopped unsalted pistachios, dried apricots, soaked couscous and torn fresh mint leaves into the carrot mix.

METHOD:

Preheat the oven to 400°F. Drain and rinse the chickpeas, then spread out on a baking sheet. Mix with a little oil and season with salt and pepper. Roast for 10–15 minutes until crisp, shaking the baking sheet every 5 minutes or so. Cool.

While the chickpeas are roasting, peel the carrots and cut into matchsticks. Set aside.

Toast the cumin/fennel seeds in a dry, medium-sized frying pan for about 3 minutes over medium heat until fragrant. Smash into a powder with a mortar and pestle or the back of a rolling pin. Tip the spice powder back into the pan and add the carrots, kale and a little oil. Fry for 10–15 minutes until the carrots and kale are softening but still crunchy. Keep stirring as they fry.

Whisk together the dressing ingredients with a fork.

To pack: Toss the chickpeas and carrrot mix with the dressing and parsley and season with salt and pepper, then pack into the lunchboxes. Crumble the feta on top.

CARROT, PARMESAN, ARUGULA, LENTIL + CHILI PEPPER SALAD

INGREDIENTS:

½ cup green lentils
6 carrots
olive oil
2 cups arugula
⅓ cup Parmesan shavings

Dressing
1 fresh red chili pepper
1 tablespoon honey
1 tablespoon cider vinegar
lemon juice

TRY THIS…

· Add a few pieces of crispy chorizo/bacon.

· Swap the honey for maple syrup.

· Add a finely sliced raw red onion.

METHOD:

Preheat the oven to 400°F. Put the lentils in a pan, add 1 cup water and bring to a simmer over medium-high heat. Cook for 15–20 minutes until al dente; drain.

Meanwhile, peel the carrots and cut into chunky matchsticks. Spread onto a baking sheet. Mix through a little olive oil and seasoning. Roast for 25 minutes until golden brown, stirring every 5 minutes or so.

To make the dressing, finely chop the chili pepper, discarding the seeds. Combine in a bowl with the honey and vinegar. Add 2–3 tablespoons olive oil and lemon juice to taste. Season.

To pack: Mix the lentils with the carrots and spoon into lunchboxes. Top with the arugula and Parmesan. Pack the dressing separately.

SMOKED FISH + CARROT SALAD
WITH HARISSA-YOGURT DRESSING

INGREDIENTS:

2 smoked fish fillets (such as trout, hot-smoked
    salmon or mackerel)
6 carrots
2 handfuls of mixed dried fruit (raisins, apricots,
    figs, and/or cranberries)
2½ cups mixed greens
⅓ cup toasted sliced almonds

Harissa dressing
2 teaspoons harissa paste
1 tablespoon Greek yogurt
juice of ½ lemon
1 tablespoon olive oil

METHOD:

Chop or tear the fish into big pieces and set
aside. Depending on what fish you choose,
remove any skin or visible bones as needed.

Peel and grate the carrots. Cut the dried fruit
into small pieces.

Whisk together all the dressing ingredients with
2 tablespoons water.

To pack: Line the lunchboxes with the greens and
top with the carrots, fish, fruit and almonds. Pack
the dressing separately.

TRY THIS...

· Swap the harissa for horseradish cream/one of
  our pestos (*see pages 154–155*).

· Replace the fish with chicken breast strips fried
  in a little oil for 5 minutes.

· Add 2 chopped boiled sweet potatoes, peeled,
  cut into large chunks and boiled for 6 minutes.

CARROT + ZUCCHINI RIBBON SALAD WITH HONEY + ORANGE CHICKEN

INGREDIENTS:

2 skinless boneless chicken breasts
coconut/olive oil
1 tablespoon honey
2 oranges
⅓ cup crushed peanuts/sliced almonds/
    mixed seeds
5 carrots
2 zucchini

Dressing
1½ tablespoons honey
2 tablespoons soy sauce
1 orange, juiced

METHOD:

Preheat the oven to 400°F. Place the chicken on a baking sheet. Drizzle over a little oil and the honey. Zest the oranges directly on top. Season with salt and pepper. Sprinkle the nuts alongside the chicken on the same tray. Bake for 18–20 minutes until the chicken is cooked through and the nuts are golden brown. Cool, then slice the chicken.

While the chicken is in the oven, remove the white part from two of the oranges and slice into ½-inch-thick discs. Peel the carrots and slice into ribbons with a peeler. Repeat with the zucchini but discard the watery center.

Whisk together the ingredients for the dressing with the juice from the third orange.

To pack: Spread the vegetable ribbons in the lunchboxes. Add a layer of orange slices and top with the sliced chicken and nuts. Pack the dressing separately.

TRY THIS…

· Swap the zucchini or carrots for ribbons of cooked and peeled beet.

· Add a cup of cooked quinoa and a handful of chopped fresh herbs.

CHICKEN CARROT COCONUT SALAD

INGREDIENTS:

2 skinless boneless chicken breasts
3 tablespoons dried shredded coconut
coconut/olive oil
5 carrots
2½ cups arugula
2 handfuls of pomegranate seeds
2 portions of Coconut-lime Dressing
   (see page 153)

TRY THIS...

Swap the chicken for cooked peeled shrimp.

METHOD:

Preheat the oven to 400°F. Place the chicken on a baking sheet. Sprinkle over the shredded coconut and add a splash of oil and a pinch of salt. Bake for 18–20 minutes until cooked through. Cool, then slice at an angle.

While the chicken is cooking, peel the carrots and spiralize (or slice into strips with a peeler).

To pack: Place the spiralized carrots in one half of the lunchboxes and the arugula in the other half. Fan the sliced chicken across the arugula and carrot. Sprinkle over the pomegranate seeds. Pack the dressing separately.

CARROT NOODLES + PEANUT TERIYAKI SALMON

INGREDIENTS:

2 skinless salmon fillets, about 4–6 oz. each
2 tablespoons roughly chopped fresh cilantro
olive oil
2 tablespoons sesame seeds
4 carrots
2 zucchini
2 portions of Peanut Teriyaki Sauce *(see page 156)*

METHOD:

Preheat the oven to 400°F. Place the salmon on a foil-lined baking sheet. Mix together the cilantro, a splash of olive oil and the sesame seeds. Spread over the salmon. Bake for 12 minutes. Cool.

Meanwhile, peel the carrots and spiralize. Trim the zucchini and spiralize. Place both in a bowl and toss together.

To pack: Place the carrot and zucchini noodles in the lunchboxes and lay the salmon fillets across them. Pack the Peanut Teriyaki Sauce separately.

CARROT RIBBON, CHICKEN + POMEGRANATE QUINOA TABBOULEH

INGREDIENTS:

²/₃ cup quinoa
2 skinless boneless chicken breasts
olive oil
6 spring onions or scallions (white bulbs and
    most of green)
10 cherry tomatoes
4 carrots
2 tablespoons finely chopped fresh mixed herbs
    (parsley, mint, chives)
2 handfuls of pomegranate seeds
lemon juice

TRY THIS…

Add roasted sweet potato cubes, crumbled feta
and crushed red pepper instead of (or as well as)
chicken and pomegranate.

METHOD:

Put the quinoa, 1¹/₃ cups water and a pinch of salt
in a medium pot and bring to a boil. Reduce heat
to low, cover and simmer 15–20 minutes until the
liquid has been absorbed. Fluff with a fork.

While the quinoa is cooking, finely slice the
chicken and place in a frying pan with a little
oil and seasoning. Finely slice the spring onions
and add to the pan. Fry over medium-high heat
for 7–10 minutes until the chicken is cooked
through, stirring frequently.

Combine the quinoa, chicken and spring onions
in a bowl. Cool.

Halve the cherry tomatoes. Peel the carrots and
slice into ribbons with a peeler. Add the tomatoes
and carrots to the bowl, then mix through the
herbs and pomegranate seeds. Season to taste
with salt, pepper, lemon juice and olive oil.

To pack: Spoon into two lunchboxes.

CHOPPED SOBA MISO SALAD

INGREDIENTS:

METHOD:

4 oz. soba noodles

¾ cup frozen shelled edamame beans

4 carrots

¼ red cabbage

2 spring onions or scallions (white bulbs and
   most of the green part)

2 tablespoons sesame seeds

4 teaspoons miso paste

2 limes

Bring a large pot of water to a boil. Add soba
noodles and cook 5–8 minutes or according to
package directions until al dente. Drain and rinse
in cold water to cool quickly, then roughly chop
up using kitchen scissors.

While the noodles are cooking, put the
edamame in a bowl of cold water and set aside
to thaw for 5 minutes; drain. Peel the carrots
and spiralize. Remove the tough outer leaves
and core from the red cabbage, then thinly slice.
Thinly slice the spring onions at an angle. Toast
the sesame seeds in a small pan over medium
heat until golden.

Put the miso in a bowl. Zest the limes into the
bowl and squeeze in the juice. Add a splash of
hot water and mix well.

To pack: Arrange the vegetables and noodles
in the lunchboxes (or mix them together)
and sprinkle the toasted sesame seeds on top.
Pack the dressing separately.

TOMATO

HERB + NUT-STUFFED TOMATOES

INGREDIENTS:

1 cup quinoa
6 medium beefsteak tomatoes
2 garlic cloves
coconut/olive oil
4 cups baby spinach leaves
2 tablespoons each roughly chopped
   fresh parsley and mint
1 lemon
2/3 cup chopped mixed nuts (e.g., hazelnuts,
   unsalted cashew and walnuts)
1/2 cup grated mozzarella

TRY THIS...

· Add 2 handfuls of pulled chicken *(see page 30)* or diced cooked sausages to the quinoa.

· Experiment with different herbs such as chervil and chives.

METHOD:

Preheat the oven to 350°F. Put the quinoa in a medium pot with 2 cups water and a pinch of salt and bring to a boil. Reduce heat to low, cover and simmer 15 minutes until the liquid has been absorbed. Fluff with a fork.

While the quinoa is cooking, slice the top off each tomato and scoop out the seeds and fleshy part (don't throw this away). Carefully slice a very thin layer off the bottom of each tomato to make sure it will sit upright. Place the tomatoes on a baking sheet lined with parchment paper. Set aside.

Peel and finely dice the garlic. Place in a pan with a splash of oil and cook over medium heat for 2 minutes. Add the tomato seeds/flesh, 3 cups of the baby spinach and the herbs. Cook for 5 minutes, stirring constantly.

Add the cooked quinoa to the pan, season and stir well. Cook for a further 3–5 minutes. Zest the lemon into the pan and add the juice too, with a splash of water if the mix starts to stick.

Toast the mixed nuts in a dry pan over medium heat until golden brown. Chop the nuts, then mix half into the quinoa. Divide the quinoa mix among the tomatoes. Cover the baking sheet with foil and bake for 15 minutes.

Top the tomatoes with the grated mozzarella and remaining chopped nuts, then bake for a further 5 minutes.

To pack: Allow the tomatoes to cool, then place carefully, side by side, in the lunchboxes and pile the remaining spinach leaves on top.

TOM YUM SOUP

INGREDIENTS:

1 small white onion

2–3 fresh red birds' eye chilies (optional)

coconut/olive oil

rice wine vinegar (optional)

a flavor bundle: 2 lemongrass stalks, 4 kaffir
   lime leaves (or 2 chopped limes) and 1 small
   piece galangal root (or fresh ginger), peeled
   and roughly chopped, all wrapped together in
   muslin or cheesecloth and tied with a length of
   string so it is easy to remove later

½ x 14-oz. can coconut milk

8 medium tomatoes

2 red peppers

2 zucchini

lime juice

soy sauce

chopped fresh cilantro

METHOD:

Peel and finely dice the onion (and chilies, if
using). Place in a pan with a splash of oil and
cook over a medium heat for 3 minutes. Add a
splash of rice wine vinegar (if using) and cook for
another minute. Add the flavor bundle, coconut
milk and 1 cup boiling water and cook for
another 5 minutes.

Meanwhile, dice the tomatoes into ½-inch cubes.
Remove the core and seeds from the peppers,
then cut, along with the zucchini, into cubes
similar in size to the tomatoes. Add all these
vegetables to the pan and continue to cook for
8 minutes over medium heat. Stir occasionally.

Remove from the heat. Discard the flavor bundle.
Season the soup with lime juice, soy sauce and
chopped cilantro to taste.

To pack: Cool, then pour into watertight
containers, to prevent leakage.

TRY THIS...

· Add raw peeled shrimp or prawns for the final
   few minutes of cooking and simmer until they
   turn pink.

· Bulk this up with more vegetables. Broccoli
   works really well—add to the pan at the same
   time as the tomatoes, zucchini and red peppers.

SAMBOL RYE

INGREDIENTS:

1 red onion
coconut/olive oil
2 teaspoons ground ginger
2 teaspoons chili powder
4 tablespoons dried shredded coconut
2 beefsteak tomatoes
1 handful of cherry tomatoes
2 slices rye bread
3 cups arugula/baby spinach leaves
2 lemon wedges (optional)

METHOD:

Peel and finely dice the red onion. Place in a pan with a splash of oil and cook over medium heat for 3–4 minutes. Stir in the ground ginger and chili powder and cook for another 2 minutes. Remove from the heat.

In another pan toast the shredded coconut over medium heat until golden. Add half of the coconut to the onions.

Roughly dice the tomatoes and add to the onions. Return to the heat and cook for 3–4 minutes until the tomatoes start to break down. Season and cool.

Slice the cherry tomatoes in half.

To pack: Place the rye bread on the bottom of the lunchboxes. Top with a layer of half the arugula/spinach, followed by the onion and tomato mixture (this arrangement prevents the rye from going soggy). Scatter the halved cherry tomatoes and the remaining toasted coconut and arugula/spinach over the top. Tuck a wedge of lemon into each lunchbox, if using.

HARISSA, TOMATO + MOZZARELLA SALAD

INGREDIENTS:

1 pint of cherry tomatoes (a mixture of colors
  works well)
1 handful of fresh basil leaves
1 handful of fresh parsley
1 cucumber
15–20 small mozzarella pearls

Harissa dressing
2–3 teaspoons harissa paste
juice of ½ lemon
2 tablespoons olive oil
2 teaspoons honey or sugar

TRY THIS…

· Replace the harissa with one of our pestos
  (see pages 154–155) or tahini.

· Add an avocado, diced, or a few slices of
  prosciutto, torn into pieces.

METHOD:

Mix all the ingredients for the dressing together
with 1 tablespoon water and season with salt
and pepper.

Slice the tomatoes in half and place in a bowl.
Tear over the basil. Finely chop the parsley and
sprinkle on top.

Slice the cucumber in half lengthways and scoop
out the seeds with a teaspoon. Cut across into
chunks on an angle. Add to the bowl along with
the mozzarella. Mix everything together.

To pack: Spoon the salad into the lunchboxes.
Pack the dressing separately.

RIBOLATA SALAD

INGREDIENTS:

2½ cups chopped kale
2 carrots
1 zucchini
1 leek
olive oil
1 teaspoon crushed red pepper
1 x 15.5-oz. can cannellini beans
4 tablespoons chopped mixed fresh herbs
2 handfuls of mixed cherry tomatoes

METHOD:

Boil a large pot of water. Place the kale in a bowl, cover with boiled water and leave for 5 minutes. Drain and rinse under cold water.

While the kale is blanching, peel the carrots and slice into very thin rounds. Slice the zucchini into very thin rounds. Slice the leek into ¼-inch-thick rounds.

Put the leek in a frying pan with a glug of olive oil, a pinch of salt and the crushed red pepper flakes and cook over medium heat, stirring frequently, for 5 minutes until soft. Tip into a bowl and add the carrots and zucchini. Season.

Add the kale, drained and rinsed beans, herbs and sliced cherry tomatoes. Toss together gently.

To pack: Spoon into the lunchboxes.

TRY THIS...

· Add 2 handfuls of pulled chicken *(see page 30)*.

· Top with a dollop of Green Pesto *(see page 154)*.

TIP: Ribolata is a hearty Tuscan soup that is great for using up leftovers. We have turned the common ingredients into a salad here.

TOMATO, SAUSAGE + BUTTER BEAN SALAD

4 pork or beef sausages
olive oil
1 tablespoon smoked paprika
1 teaspoon crushed red pepper
1 x 15.5-oz. can butter beans
2 tablespoons chopped fresh mixed herbs (basil and parsley work well)
2 red peppers
10 cherry tomatoes
2 tablespoons balsamic vinegar (optional)

Using scissors, cut the sausages into 1-inch discs. Place in a pan with a splash of oil, the smoked paprika and crushed red pepper and fry over medium-low heat for 10–15 minutes until browned all over and cooked through. Cool.

While the sausages are cooking, drain and rinse the butter beans. Toss them with the fresh herbs and season with a pinch of salt.

Remove the core and seeds from the red peppers, then cut into chunky pieces. Halve the cherry tomatoes. Mix the peppers and tomatoes with the sausage and drizzle with balsamic vinegar.

To pack: Spoon the sausage mix into one side of each lunchbox alongside the herby butter beans.

TRY THIS… Replace the sausages with chorizo, removed from casings—omit the paprika and crushed red pepper, and cook for 5–8 minutes.

CANDIED MISO TOMATO SALAD

6 strips of bacon
2½ cups chopped kale
⅓ cup pecans
2 tablespoons honey, plus extra for drizzling
4 teaspoons miso paste
2 teaspoons ginger paste
3 handfuls of cherry tomatoes

Preheat the oven to 400°F and boil a pot of water. Lay the bacon strips on a foil-lined baking sheet and bake for 10–15 minutes until crisp.

Meanwhile, place the kale in a bowl and cover with boiling water. Leave for 5 minutes, then drain and rinse under cold water. Set to one side.

While the bacon and kale are baking/blanching, place the pecans in a frying pan and lightly toast over medium heat for 2 minutes until golden. Add a drizzle of honey and briefly toss the nuts until caramelized. Pour onto a sheet of parchment paper and leave to cool before chopping roughly.

To make the miso dressing, put the miso, 2 tablespoons honey and the ginger paste in a pan with a splash of water (not too much as the dressing should be thick in consistency). Cook over a medium heat for 1–2 minutes until just thickening. Cool.

Slice the cherry tomatoes in half.

To pack: Line the bottom of the lunchboxes with the kale. Scatter the cherry tomatoes and pecans over the kale. Roughly break up the bacon on top. Pack the dressing separately.

RED
PEPPER

ONE-PAN LEMON CHICKEN + CHORIZO

3 bell peppers (mixed colors)
olive oil
½ lemon
2 skinless boneless chicken breasts
3–4 oz. chorizo
4 spring onions (white bulbs only) or 1 small white onion
1 fresh red chili pepper
¼ cup toasted flaked almonds
1½ cups baby spinach leaves

Remove the core and seeds from the peppers, then cut into roughly 1-inch chunks. Place in a medium-sized pan with a little olive oil and fry over low heat for 10–15 minutes until soft. Keep stirring regularly.

About 5 minutes after you start frying the peppers, cut the lemon half into chunks and squeeze the juice into the pan. Add the squeezed chunks to the pan too.

Slice the chicken breasts into thin strips and the chorizo into discs. Once the peppers have been cooking for 7 minutes, add the chicken and chorizo to the pan and cook for another 8–10 minutes over medium heat until the chicken is cooked through, stirring frequently. Discard the lemon chunks.

Finely slice the spring onions. Finely slice the chili pepper, discarding the seeds. Stir both of these through the pepper mix. Season.

To pack: Once the chicken and pepper salad is cool, spoon into the lunchboxes. Sprinkle with the flaked almonds and pile the spinach on top.

TRY THIS… Add a can of butter beans or kidney beans, drained and rinsed.

PEANUT-DRESSED CHICKEN, BEANSPROUT + RED PEPPER SALAD

8 oz. broccolini
3 red peppers
coconut/olive oil
2 skinless boneless chicken breasts
2 cups bean sprouts
2 tablespoons finely chopped fresh cilantro
3–4 tablespoons peanut butter (preferably crunchy and sugar-free)
2 tablespoons soy sauce
1 lime

Trim the ends off the broccolini, then cut each stem in half at an angle and place in a pan. Cover with water and add a pinch of salt. Bring to a boil and cook for 3–4 minutes until al dente. Drain and rinse under cold water.

Remove the core and seeds from the red peppers, then cut into strips. Fry in a large skillet with a splash of oil for 15 minutes until very soft.

Meanwhile, slice the chicken into thin strips. Add to the peppers 5–7 minutes after the start of cooking. Keep stirring. Add the bean sprouts for the final minute of cooking. Turn into a bowl and mix in the broccolini and cilantro.

Put the peanut butter in a small pan and allow to melt over low heat. Remove from the heat. Whisk in the soy sauce. Zest the lime into the pan and add the juice too. Taste and add more soy sauce if needed plus a splash of hot water if the dressing seems too thick.

To pack: Spoon the salad into the lunchboxes. Pack the dressing separately.

TRY THIS… Serve with Coconut-lime Dressing *(see page 153)* instead.

OREGANO-BAKED FETA WITH A MEDITERRANEAN SALAD

INGREDIENTS:

4 oz. feta (or halloumi or tofu)
1 tablespoon chopped fresh oregano
    (or 2 teaspoons dried Italian herbs/
    oregano/thyme)
olive oil
4 jarred roasted red peppers (or 3 raw red
    peppers, cut into matchsticks)
2 handfuls of cherry tomatoes
1 garlic clove
1 x 15.5-oz. can butter beans/kidney beans
2 teaspoons red wine vinegar
2 tablespoons finely chopped fresh parsley

TRY THIS…

· Toast some rye bread and chop into croutons.
  Pack separately to garnish the salad.

· Add 2 sweet potatoes, peeled, cut into 1-inch
  chunks and boiled for 10 minutes.

· Stir 1 cup of cooked wild rice into the bean and
  pepper salad.

· Pile a handful of baby spinach leaves on top
  of the feta in the lunchboxes.

METHOD:

Preheat the oven to 400°F. Line a baking sheet with a piece of foil (large enough to wrap up the feta). Cut the feta into roughly 1-inch pieces and place on the foil with the oregano, some salt and pepper and a little olive oil. Mix well, then wrap up like a package. Bake for 10 minutes.

Meanwhile, cut the peppers into strips and halve the cherry tomatoes. Place these in a bowl. Peel the garlic and crush on top. Add the drained and rinsed beans, a little olive oil, the vinegar and parsley and mix thoroughly. Season with salt and pepper.

To pack: Spoon the bean and pepper salad into the lunchboxes. When the feta has cooled, arrange it on top of the salad.

RED PEPPER + EGGPLANT PASTA
WITH RED PESTO

INGREDIENTS:

1½ cups whole wheat fusilli
coconut/olive oil
1 large eggplant
2 portions of Red Pepper Pesto *(see page 155)*
3 jarred roasted red peppers
lemon juice (optional)
¼ cup toasted pine nuts
grated Parmesan/crumbled feta, to garnish
2 cups arugula

TRY THIS…

· Fry 6 oz. lean ground beef until well browned. Stir through the pasta salad before packing in the lunchboxes.

· Bake 2 cod fillets, each topped with a teaspoon of Red Pepper Pesto, in a 400°F oven for 12–15 minutes. Place the cooled fish on the pasta salad and finish with the nuts, cheese and arugula.

· Turn this into a hot gratin to eat at home: sprinkle equal amounts of grated Parmesan and breadcrumbs on top of the pasta salad in a baking dish and bake in a 400°F oven for 10–15 minutes.

METHOD:

Boil a large pot of salted water. Once boiling, add the pasta and cook according to package directions until al dente. Drain and toss with a little oil to prevent sticking.

While the pasta is cooking, remove the stalk from the eggplant then cut into ½-inch chunks. Place in a pan, cover with water and add a pinch of salt. Bring to a boil and cook for 2 minutes until the eggplant is just starting to soften. Drain and rinse under cold water.

Tip the eggplant into a frying pan and add a little oil. Fry over high heat for 4 minutes until cooked through and slightly crisp. Keep stirring. Remove from the heat and mix through the pasta with the pesto.

Finely slice the red peppers and add to the pan. Season and add a little extra oil or some lemon juice if needed.

To pack: Spoon the pasta salad into the lunchboxes. Scatter the pine nuts and cheese on the salad and top with the arugula.

RED PEPPER + FENNEL QUINOA SALAD WITH CHORIZO

INGREDIENTS:

1 cup quinoa
1 fennel bulb
2 red peppers
1 garlic clove
coconut/olive oil
3–4 oz. chorizo or Italian sausage
2 teaspoons cumin seeds
1 tablespoon honey
lemon juice

TRY THIS…

· Swap the quinoa for a 15.5-oz. can of butter beans, drained and rinsed.

· Instead of frying the fennel, use it raw.

METHOD:

Place quinoa in a pot with a pinch of salt and $1\frac{1}{2}$ cups water. Bring to a boil. Cover, reduce heat to low and simmer 15–20 minutes until the water has been absorbed. Fluff with a fork.

While the quinoa is cooking, remove the outer leaves and core from the fennel, then finely slice. Remove the core and seeds from the red peppers, then finely slice. Peel and crush the garlic. Place the fennel, red peppers and garlic in a frying pan with a little oil and fry over low heat for 10 minutes until soft. Keep stirring.

Turn up the heat to medium-high and fry for another 5 minutes until slightly crisp. Stir the pepper mix through the quinoa and set aside.

Slice the chorizo into thin discs or remove meat from casing. Fry for 5–7 minutes until brown and cooked through, adding cumin seeds for the last 2 minutes.

Mix the honey and a little lemon juice through the quinoa salad. Season with salt and pepper.

To pack: Once cool, spoon the quinoa salad into the lunchboxes and scatter the chorizo on top.

TIP: Keep the fine fennel leaves and scatter over the chorizo for extra aniseed flavor.

STUFFED PEPPERS WITH TOMATOES, COUSCOUS, + KALE + WALNUT PESTO

3 red peppers
olive oil
$\frac{1}{2}$ cup couscous
$2\frac{1}{2}$ cups chopped kale
2 handfuls of cherry tomatoes
$\frac{1}{2}$ cup walnuts
2 portions of Kale and Walnut Pesto *(see page 155)*
lemon juice (optional)

Preheat the oven to 400°F. Cut the peppers in half vertically and scoop out the seeds and white ribs. Place the halves skin side down on a baking sheet and drizzle over a little oil. Season. Bake for 25 minutes until soft.

While the peppers are in the oven, put the couscous in a bowl and cover with boiling water (the water level should be about $\frac{1}{4}$ inch above the couscous). Cover with plastic wrap and set aside for at least 5 minutes until soft.

Meanwhile, place the chopped kale in a bowl, cover with boiling water and leave for 5 minutes. Drain and rinse under cold water.

Halve the cherry tomatoes. Lightly crush the walnuts, then toast in a dry pan until golden.

Fluff up the couscous with a fork. Mix together the couscous, kale, tomatoes, walnuts and most of the pesto. Season and add lemon juice and/or olive oil to taste. Spoon into the pepper halves.

To pack: Cool the peppers before placing 3 halves in each lunchbox, in one layer. Top each with a little extra pesto.

TRY THIS… Switch the couscous to quinoa.

SPINACH + PEA-STUFFED PEPPERS WITH GOAT CHEESE

3 red peppers
olive oil
2 red onions
1 cup frozen peas
4 cups baby spinach leaves
15 fresh basil leaves
1 x 15.5-oz. can chickpeas
lemon juice
4–5 oz. soft fresh goat cheese, crumbled

Preheat the oven to 415°F. Slice the peppers in half vertically and scoop out the seeds and white ribs. Place the halves skin side down on a baking sheet. Drizzle over a little oil and season with salt and pepper, then bake for 20 minutes until soft.

Meanwhile, peel and finely slice the onions. Place in a frying pan with a splash of oil and cook over low heat for 10 minutes until completely soft. Thaw the peas in a bowl of cold water for 1–2 minutes; drain.

Add the spinach to the pan and fry for 2 minutes until wilted. Remove from the heat and stir through the peas, torn basil and drained and rinsed chickpeas. Season well, adding lemon juice and more olive oil to taste.

When the peppers are nearly ready, remove from the oven and fill generously with the spinach mixture (if you have extra you can serve it on the side). Sprinkle over the goat cheese. Place back in the oven and bake for a final 5 minutes until the cheese melts and turns slightly golden.

To pack: Cool the pepper halves before placing in the lunchboxes, in one layer.

RED PEPPER + BUTTER BEAN HUMMUS WITH ROASTED SQUASH + PARMESAN

INGREDIENTS:

1 small butternut squash
coconut/olive oil
1 fresh red chili pepper
2 jarred roasted red peppers
2 cups mixed greens
1/3 cup Parmesan shavings
1/2 lemon
2 portions of Red Pepper and
    Butter Bean Hummus *(see page 157)*

TRY THIS…

· Add 1–2 teaspoons harissa paste to the hummus.

· Swap the jarred peppers for 2 raw red peppers, cut into strips and roasted with the squash.

METHOD:

Preheat the oven to 400°C. Peel the squash and cut into chunks or sticks about 1/4-inch thick, discarding the seeds. Place in a pan, cover with water and add a pinch of salt. Bring to a boil and cook for 3 minutes.

Drain the squash and place on a baking sheet. Drizzle over a little oil and season with salt and pepper. Roast for 20 minutes, flipping the pieces over halfway through cooking. Cool.

While the squash is roasting, finely dice the chili pepper, discarding the seeds. Slice the red peppers into strips.

To pack: Mix the greens with the Parmesan shavings and diced chili pepper and pile on one side of the lunchboxes. Pile the peppers and squash on the other side. Tuck a wedge of lemon into each box. Pack the hummus separately.

PADRÓN PEPPER, CHORIZO + HALLOUMI SALAD

INGREDIENTS:

¾ cup quinoa (black works well here)
1 lime
2 spring onions or scallions (white bulbs and most
    of the green)
2 tablespoons chopped fresh cilantro
coconut/olive oil
a mixture of peppers such as 5 Padrón or
    shishito peppers and 5 small sweet peppers
sea salt
3–4 oz. chorizo
4–6 oz. halloumi
2½ cups arugula

TRY THIS…

If you can't find Padrón or small sweet peppers,
you can use 5 regular peppers, each cut into
4 big wedges or "boats." Fry, then fill them with
the quinoa mix.

METHOD:

Put the quinoa in a pan with 1½ cups water and
a pinch of salt. Bring to a boil, then cover, reduce
heat to low and simmer for 15–20 minutes until
the water has been absorbed. Fluff with a fork,
then zest in the lime and add the juice too. Mix
through the spring onions and cilantro.

While the quinoa is cooking, heat a frying pan
with a splash of oil, add the whole peppers and
fry over medium heat until they have browned
and blistered. Tip into a bowl and season with
sea salt. Set aside.

Slice the chorizo into ½-inch-thick rounds and
the halloumi into small chunks. Heat another
frying pan with a splash of oil. Add the chorizo
and sauté for 5 minutes or until crisp. Partway
through, add the halloumi and cook for a few
minutes on each side until golden.

To pack: Spoon the quinoa salad into the
lunchboxes and top with the peppers, chorizo
and halloumi. Scatter arugula over the top of
the salad.

GENERAL BEET NOTES

1. To save time, these recipes are all made with precooked peeled beets. For best flavor, look for sealed or vacuum-packed precooked beets, rather than canned beets, at your supermarket.

2. You can also make your own steamed beets ahead of time and keep them in your fridge until ready to use. Slice off the greens and scrub the beets clean. Place in a steamer basket over 2 inches of water. Bring to a boil, cover, reduce heat to medium and steam the beets for 30 minutes until tender. Remove from heat. When cool enough to handle, remove the skins and ends. Keep covered in the refrigerator for 3–4 days.

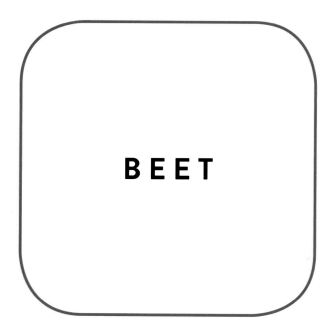

BEET

BEET CORONATION CHICKEN

INGREDIENTS:

2 skinless boneless chicken breasts
1 tablespoon coconut oil
2 tablespoons curry powder
2 teaspoons tomato purée
8 cooked and peeled beets
1 cucumber
1 lemon
4 tablespoons Greek yogurt
about 2 tablespoons honey, to taste
1/2 cup toasted sliced almonds

TRY THIS…

· Garnish with a small handful of chopped fresh
  cilantro or chopped dried apricots/cranberries.

· Serve for dinner with a roasted sweet potato
  and spinach leaves.

METHOD:

Preheat the oven to 400°F. Line a baking sheet
with foil or parchment then place the chicken
breasts on the pan, rub them with coconut oil,
curry powder, the tomato purée and a pinch of
salt. Bake in the oven for 18–20 minutes. Allow
to cool then slice at an angle.

While the chicken is cooling, cut the beets
into 1/2-inch cubes. Slice the cucumber in half
lengthways and scoop out the seeds with a metal
spoon. Slice the halves in half lengthways, then
finely dice.

Put the beet and cucumber in a bowl. Zest and
juice the lemon and add with the yogurt and a
little honey. Mix and season with salt and pepper.
Add more honey to taste.

To pack: Spoon the salad into one side of the
lunchboxes and the chicken into the other
(or gently fold the chicken into the salad first).
Sprinkle the almonds on top.

BALSAMIC, BEET + RED ONION SALAD WITH GOAT CHEESE

INGREDIENTS:

2 red onions
6–8 cooked and peeled beets
1 x 15.5-oz. can chickpeas
½ cup mixed nuts
2 tablespoons honey
2 tablespoons balsamic vinegar
1½ cups arugula
2–3 oz. soft goat cheese

TRY THIS…

· Add some picked and chopped fresh rosemary/
  thyme to the vegetables while they roast.

· Swap the chickpeas for cooked pasta
  (preferably shell pasta, or conchiglie).

METHOD:

Preheat the oven to 400°F. Peel the onions, then chop with the beets into roughly ½-inch cubes. Pile on a baking sheet with the drained and rinsed chickpeas, roughly crushed nuts, honey and balsamic. Toss together, then spread out.

Roast for 10 minutes until everything is slightly crisp in parts. Shake the tray every few minutes to move the ingredients.

To pack: Allow to cool, then season with salt and pepper. Pack the salad in the lunchboxes and top with the arugula. Scatter lumps of goat cheese on top of the arugula.

HERBY QUINOA SALAD WITH SMOKED SALMON, PEAS + BEETS

INGREDIENTS:

¾ cup quinoa (or bulgur wheat)
6–8 cooked and peeled beets
4 slices smoked salmon
½ cup pumpkin seeds
1¼ cups frozen peas
4 tablespoons finely chopped mixed fresh herbs
  (parsley, chives, dill, mint and/or chervil)
juice of ½ lemon
olive oil

TRY THIS...

· Stir in a tablespoon of one of our pestos (*see pages 154–155*) with the oil at the end.

· Add a handful each of blueberries and unsalted cashew nuts instead of smoked salmon.

· Swap the smoked salmon for a baked trout fillet. Place the trout on a baking sheet, sprinkle with a splash of oil and pinch of salt, and bake in a 350°F oven for 12 minutes. Cool, then flake on top of the salad in the lunchboxes.

METHOD:

Put the quinoa in a pot with 1½ cups water and a pinch of salt. Bring to a boil, then cover, reduce heat to low and simmer for 15 minutes until water has absorbed. Fluff with a fork.

While the quinoa is cooking, cut the beets into small cubes. Slice the salmon into strips. Toast the pumpkin seeds in a dry pan over medium heat for 2 minutes until they start to pop.

Thaw the peas in a bowl of cold water for 1–2 minutes; drain. Mix the peas, herbs and lemon juice into the quinoa.

To pack: When the quinoa is cool, fold in the beets, salmon and pumpkin seeds, then add a splash of olive oil and season to taste. Divide between the lunchboxes.

TIP: Keep herbs fresh for longer in the fridge by covering loosely with a slightly damp tea towel or paper towel.

ORANGE + BEET SALAD WITH
ORANGE DRESSING

INGREDIENTS:

½ cup green lentils
6–8 cooked and peeled beets
4 oranges
⅓ cup sliced almonds
⅓ cup walnuts
2½ cups arugula

Orange shallot dressing
2 shallots/1 small white onion
1 tablespoon olive oil
1 tablespoon honey
juice of 2 oranges
1 tablespoon red wine vinegar/cider vinegar

TRY THIS…

· Top with some crumbled goat cheese and
a ready-made balsamic glaze.

· Add salmon: place a 4–6 oz. salmon fillet in a
small baking dish and top with a tablespoon
of honey or maple syrup and some orange zest,
then bake in a 400°F oven for 12 minutes.
Cool before placing on the salad (whole or
flaked) and top with arugula.

METHOD:

Preheat the oven to 400°F. Put the lentils in a
pan, add 1 cup water and bring to a simmer over
medium-high heat. Cook for 15–20 minutes until
al dente. Drain.

While the lentils are cooking, slice the beets into
thin discs. Repeat with the oranges, picking out
any seeds. Pull off the orange peel and add to the
lentils while they cook, for extra flavor.

To make the dressing, peel and finely chop the
shallots. Tip into a small pan and fry over low
heat in the tablespoon of oil for 10 minutes until
softened. Add the rest of the dressing ingredients
and reduce over low heat until just thickened and
slightly syrupy (check by seeing how the dressing
runs off a spoon).

Toast the nuts in a dry pan over medium heat
until golden brown.

To pack: Mix all the prepared ingredients and
dressing together and cool, then pack in the
lunchboxes. Top with the arugula leaves.

TIP: Make a bigger batch of the dressing—it will keep for 5 days in the fridge.

WILD RICE + BEET KEDGEREE

INGREDIENTS:

1 cup long grain and wild rice blend
2 eggs
1 garlic clove
1 small piece fresh ginger
2 spring onions (white bulbs only)
coconut/olive oil
2 teaspoons curry powder
½ cup frozen shelled edamame beans
6 cooked and peeled beets
1½ cups baby spinach leaves
4 tablespoons Greek yogurt (optional)
juice of 1 lemon

METHOD:

Preheat the oven to 400°F. Put the rice mix in a pan with 1½ cups water and a pinch of salt. Cover and bring to a boil, then reduce heat and simmer for 25 minutes or according to package directions until al dente.

While the rice is cooking, put the eggs in another pan and cover with cold water by 1 inch. Bring to a boil over medium-high heat, then cover, remove from heat and set aside 8–10 minutes to hard boil. Rinse under cold water, then peel and cut in half.

Peel the garlic and crush into a frying pan. Peel the ginger and grate into the pan. Finely chop the spring onions and add to the pan along with a little oil. Fry over medium heat for 2 minutes, stirring. Stir in the curry powder and fry for another 2 minutes. Remove from the heat.

Thaw the edamame in a bowl of cold water for 1–2 minutes; drain.

Finely chop the beets and stir in the spice base along with the rice, spinach, edamame and yogurt. Add lemon juice to taste and season.

To pack: Once the kedgeree is cool, pack into the lunchboxes and set the egg halves on top.

TRY THIS...

Add salmon. Dress 2 x 4-oz. salmon fillets with a little grating of fresh ginger, a sprinkle of turmeric and salt and a drizzle of olive oil, then bake in a 400°F oven for 12 minutes. Cool. Flake and fold through the salad.

BEETROOT HUMMUS WITH WILD RICE + KALE

INGREDIENTS:

1 cup long grain and wild rice blend
2½ cups chopped kale
10 breakfast radishes
1 cucumber
10 fresh mint leaves
1 lemon
2 portions of Beetroot Hummus *(see page 157)*
2 tablespoons mixed seeds (optional)

TRY THIS…

Add smoked or baked salmon. Place a 4-oz. salmon fillet on a baking sheet and bake in a 400°F oven for 12 minutes. Cool, then flake over the salad.

METHOD:

Put the rice mix in a pan with 1½ cups water and add a pinch of salt. Cover and bring to a boil, then reduce heat and simmer 25 minutes or according to package directions until al dente. Tip into a bowl.

While the rice is cooking, put the chopped kale in a bowl, cover with boiling water and leave for 5 minutes. Drain and rinse under cold water. Remove the stalks from the radishes, then slice in half lengthways. Cut the cucumber in half lengthways and scoop out the seeds with a teaspoon. Slice each half across into spears.

Roughly chop the mint and add to the rice. Zest and juice the lemon and add to the rice. Season and toss together with a little olive oil.

To pack: Put the rice in one half of the lunchboxes. Place the kale in the other half. On top of the kale, arrange the radishes on one half and the cucumber on the other. Dollop the hummus in one corner of the rice. Sprinkle the rice with the mixed seeds.

SPIRALIZED BEET VEGETABLE RAGU

INGREDIENTS:

4 oz. green beans
2 cups chopped kale
6–8 cooked and peeled beets
½ red onion
20 cherry tomatoes
1 zucchini
2 tablespoons balsamic vinegar
coconut/olive oil
20 fresh basil leaves

TRY THIS…

· Any spiralized vegetable will work—spiralized butternut squash, for example.

· Finish with a sprinkling of feta.

METHOD:

Preheat the oven to 375°F.

Trim the green beans. Place in a bowl with the kale and cover with boiling water. Leave for 5 minutes, then drain.

Meanwhile, spiralize the beets. Place on a baking sheet. Add the drained beans and kale.

Peel and roughly chop the onion. Add to the baking sheet. Cut the cherry tomatoes in half. Slice the zucchini into medium-sized rounds. Add both to the baking sheet.

Sprinkle over the balsamic vinegar, a splash of oil and a pinch of salt and toss everything together. Spread out, then roast for 10–12 minutes until just cooked through.

To pack: Cool before packing in the lunchboxes. Scatter the torn basil leaves on top.

GOAT CHEESE TOAST WITH BEETROOT HUMMUS

INGREDIENTS:

1 lemon
2–3 oz. soft goat cheese
20 fresh chives
2 slices rye bread
2 portions of Beetroot Hummus *(see page 157)*
2½ cups arugula
⅓ cup mixed seeds

TRY THIS…

Pack some smoked salmon too, and pile onto the goat cheese toasts before eating.

METHOD:

Zest the lemon into a bowl and add the goat cheese. Finely chop the chives and add. Mix well.

Toast the rye bread. Cut each slice into quarters.

To pack: Wrap/pack all the elements separately in the lunchboxes. To eat, top half of the toasts with goat cheese and the rest with beetroot hummus. Serve with the arugula and seeds.

NO-COOK BEET, ORANGE + GINGER SOUP

INGREDIENTS:

10–12 cooked and peeled beets
2 oranges (or 1 cup orange juice)
about 2 teaspoons honey, to taste
1 small piece fresh ginger, to taste

TRY THIS...

· Add a carrot for extra sweetness.

· The soup can be served hot or cold, and it
works well for breakfast if you want a vegetable
hit in the morning. To heat, use a microwave
(about 2 minutes; do not boil).

· If you have a powerful blender you can blitz
part of the peel and seeds of the orange too.
The result will be more bitter so you may want
extra honey.

METHOD:

Put the beet in a blender or juicer. Zest and juice
the orange and add along with the honey. Peel
and finely grate half the ginger and add to the
blender.

Blitz for 3–5 minutes until completely smooth.
Thin out with water (about 1 cup) to reach the
desired consistency. Taste and add more honey
or ginger, if wished.

To pack: Pour into leakproof containers.

4 IDEAS FOR BAKED EGGPLANT WITH CHICKPEAS

INGREDIENTS:

1 eggplant
1 x 15.5-oz. can chickpeas
1 cup cooked wild rice (optional)
2 cups baby spinach leaves
coconut/olive oil for drizzling
plus ingredients for one of the flavoring options
   (*see opposite and overleaf*)

METHOD:

Preheat the oven to 400°F. Remove the stalk and chop the (unpeeled) eggplant into 1-inch cubes. Place in a pan with a pinch of salt, cover with water, then bring to a boil and cook for 4 minutes until just softening. Drain and place on a baking sheet.

Mix with the drained and rinsed chickpeas plus the main ingredients for one of the flavorings. Bake for 20–25 minutes until the chickpeas are slightly crisp and the eggplant is cooked through, stirring every 5 minutes.

Allow to cool before mixing through the rice, if using, plus any extras suggested for the flavoring. Season with salt and pepper.

To pack: Spoon into the lunchboxes and pile the spinach on top. Pack the oil separately, to drizzle over before eating.

Tahini, yogurt and pomegranate

1 garlic clove
1 tablespoon honey
1 tablespoon coconut/olive oil
1 tablespoon chopped fresh parsley, optional
1 tablespoon tahini
1 tablespoon Greek yogurt
2 handfuls of pomegranate seeds

Peel and crush the garlic and add to the eggplant with the honey and oil before baking. Stir through the parsley, tahini, yogurt and pomegranate seeds once the eggplant mix has cooled.

Miso and chili

juice of 2 limes
1 tablespoon miso paste (mix with a little water so it has a sauce-like consistency)
1 teaspoon crushed red pepper
2 teaspoons honey
1 tablespoon coconut/olive oil
1 handful of chopped fresh cilantro, optional

Add the lime juice, miso paste, crushed red pepper, honey and oil to the eggplant before baking. Stir in the cilantro once the eggplant mix has cooled.

Sesame, cranberry and orange

2 oranges
2 tablespoons honey
¼ cup sesame seeds
extra: ⅓ cup dried cranberries

Zest and juice the oranges. Add to the eggplant
with the honey and sesame seeds before baking.
Stir through the cranberries once the eggplant
mix has cooled.

Tamarind, almond and ginger

1 small piece fresh ginger
2 tablespoons tamarind paste (or 1 tablespoon
   brown sugar and the juice of 1 lime)
¼ cup sliced almonds
2 teaspoons honey
1 tablespoon coconut/olive oil
extra: 20 fresh mint leaves

Peel and finely grate the ginger, then add
to the eggplant along with the tamarind
paste, almonds, honey and oil before baking.
Stir in the torn mint leaves after the eggplant
mix has cooled.

BABAGANOUSH ON RYE

2 eggplants
coconut/olive oil for drizzling
3 red peppers
4 slices rye bread
1 garlic clove
1 lemon
2 tablespoons tahini
2 tablespoons roughly chopped fresh parsley
2½ cups arugula

Preheat the oven to 425°F.

Peel the eggplants. Roughly chop into large chunks. Place in a pan, cover with water and bring to a boil, then simmer over medium heat for 3–4 minutes. Drain and place on a baking sheet. Toss with a drizzle of oil and sprinkle of salt, then roast for 5–10 minutes until golden.

Meanwhile, prepare the red peppers. Remove the core and seeds, then slice into ½-inch wedges. Place on a separate baking sheet, drizzle over some oil and season with salt. Roast for 10 minutes.

Toast the rye bread. Very finely chop the garlic; zest and juice the lemon.

Once the eggplant is ready, blitz it in a food processor until just smooth but still with some texture. Stir in the garlic, lemon zest and juice, tahini and parsley. Season.

To pack: Spoon the Babaganoush into a small container. Pack it, the oven-roasted red peppers and arugula separate from the rye bread in the lunchboxes to prevent it from going soggy. To eat, top the rye with the Babaganoush and serve the red pepper and arugula alongside.

RATATOUILLE SALAD

2 eggplants
3 zucchini
olive oil for drizzling
2 handfuls of cherry tomatoes
2 jarred roasted red peppers
1 red onion
4 tablespoons chopped mixed fresh herbs
    (e.g., mint, parsley and chives)
2½ cups mixed greens
2 tablespoons balsamic vinegar
    (or a homemade glaze, *see below*)

Heat a griddle pan over very high heat. Meanwhile, slice the eggplants lengthways into thin strips, and cut the zucchini into thin rounds. Sear the zucchini and eggplants, in batches, for about a minute until charred on each side. As they are charred, remove them to a bowl. Add a drizzle of olive oil and pinch of salt.

Cut the cherry tomatoes in half. Drain the red peppers and slice into strips. Place these in a separate bowl and season with a pinch of salt.

Peel and finely slice the onion. Add to the tomatoes and red pepper strips along with the chopped herbs.

To pack: Put the charred zucchini and eggplant in one third of each lunchbox, the greens in another third and the cherry tomato mix in the final third. Pack the balsamic vinegar separately, to be poured over the tomatoes, pepper and red onion before eating.

TRY THIS… To make a balsamic glaze, put 4 tablespoons balsamic vinegar in a pan with a little honey and reduce over low heat until sticky. Wait for the glaze to cool before drizzling over the tomatoes, red pepper and red onion (do this the night before).

EGGPLANT + ALMOND FALAFEL SALAD

INGREDIENTS:

2 eggplants
olive oil for drizzling
about 6 tablespoons ground almonds
1 tablespoon smoked paprika
1 tablespoon plus 1 teaspoon ground cumin
2 x 15.5-oz. cans chickpeas
3 cups chopped kale
2 tablespoons pumpkin seeds
1½ tablespoons tahini
4 tablespoons Greek yogurt
lemon juice

METHOD:

Preheat the oven to 425°F.

Prepare, boil and roast the eggplants as for the Babaganoush (*see opposite*). Cool slightly, then tip into a bowl and add the ground almonds, smoked paprika and 1 tablespoon cumin.

Drain and rinse the chickpeas. Put half of them in a food processor and pulse to a chunky consistency. Scrape into the bowl of eggplant. Mix well and season with a pinch of salt. Roll the mix into golfball-sized balls, adding more ground almonds if the mixture is too soft. Place the balls on a parchment-lined baking sheet and bake for 10–15 minutes until golden. Once the falafel are in the oven, spread out the remaining chickpeas on another baking sheet and toss with a splash of oil, a pinch of salt and the remaining teaspoon of cumin. Roast alongside the falafel for 8–10 minutes. Allow to cool.

Meanwhile, place the kale in a bowl, cover with boiling water and leave for 5 minutes. Drain and rinse under cold water. Set to one side.

Toast the pumpkin seeds in a dry pan over medium heat for 2 minutes until they start to pop. Make the dressing by mixing together the tahini, yogurt and lemon juice to taste with a pinch of salt.

To pack: Once all the elements of the salad have cooled, lay the kale along the bottom of the lunchboxes. Top one side with the falafel, and the other side with the roasted chickpeas. Sprinkle the toasted pumpkin seeds over everything. Pack the dressing separately.

TRY THIS…

· Add 2 handfuls of pomegranate seeds (sprinkle on top with the pumpkin seeds) and tuck in a wedge of lime.

· Serve with a chicken breast. Place a skinless, boneless chicken breast on a baking sheet and add a drizzle of oil, some chopped fresh mint and cilantro and a pinch of salt. Bake in a preheated 400°F oven for 18–20 minutes. Cool, then slice at an angle before adding to the lunchboxes.

GENERAL CAULIFLOWER NOTES

1. One small to medium cauliflower—roughly 1 or 1½ pounds once outer leaves and green parts are removed—creates 2 portions.

2. To make cauli rice, only blitz (on the pulse setting) a handful at a time for less than 30 seconds. There will still be a few small chunks. Scoop out the bits that look like rice and re-blitz what remains or chop into small pieces.

CAULI-FLOWER

CAULIFLOWER + CHERRY TOMATO SALAD
WITH ROMESCO SAUCE

INGREDIENTS:

1 small cauliflower *(see note 1, page 88)*
2 handfuls of cherry tomatoes
2 tablespoons picked fresh parsley leaves

Romesco sauce
2 thick slices day-old bread
½ cup blanched almonds (sliced work well too)
10 cherry tomatoes
1 teaspoon red wine vinegar
vegetable oil
2 jarred roasted red peppers

TRY THIS…

· Add 1 cup cooked green lentils or pile a handful of arugula on top.

· Romesco sauce will keep for 3 days in the fridge. Serve as a dip, on toast, over cooked fish or at breakfast with avocado.

· Wrap 2 skinless boneless chicken breasts in prosciutto and roast in a 400°F oven for 18–20 minutes. Serve with a dollop of Romesco and spinach leaves for dinner.

METHOD:

Preheat the oven to 400°F. To make the sauce, tear the bread into a few pieces on to a baking sheet and add half the nuts and the tomatoes. Mix in the vinegar, a little oil and season with salt and pepper. Spread out, then roast for 8–10 minutes until slightly browned all over, stirring every few minutes.

Transfer the roasted ingredients, with any cooking liquid, to a food processor. Add the red peppers, a little more oil and a splash of water. Blitz until combined. Adjust seasoning to taste. (You can add extra oil/water and blitz for longer for a smoother texture, if preferred.)

Bring a small amount of water (about 1 inch) to a boil in a saucepan. Remove the outer leaves from the cauliflower, then chop (including the base) into small florets and pieces. Put in the pan and add a pinch of salt. Cook for 3–5 minutes until al dente. Drain and rinse under cold water.

Mix the cauliflower with the halved cherry tomatoes, parsley and remaining almonds. Add seasoning.

To pack: Divide between the lunchboxes. Pack the sauce separately.

BAKED SALMON, CAULIFLOWER + TOMATO SALAD WITH BASIL DRESSING

INGREDIENTS:

2 salmon fillets, about 4–6 oz. each
vegetable oil
¼ cup pine nuts/unsalted cashews
¼ cup mixed seeds
1 small cauliflower *(see note 1, page 88)*
2 handfuls of cherry tomatoes
2 cups arugula

Basil dressing
20 fresh basil leaves
juice of 1 lemon
1 tablespoon olive oil

METHOD:

Preheat the oven to 400°F. Place the salmon on a baking sheet, drizzle over a little oil and season. Sprinkle with the nuts and seeds. Bake for 12 minutes until just cooked. Cool.

While the salmon is in the oven, remove the thick core and outer leaves from the cauliflower. Cut into small florets; cut the stalks into similar-sized chunks. Place in a pan with a pinch of salt and about an inch of water. Boil for 3–4 minutes until al dente. Drain and rinse under cold water.

Blitz the ingredients for the dressing in a food processor with 1 tablespoon water and season with salt and pepper to taste.

Cut the cherry tomatoes in half and mix with the cauliflower. If you like, flake the salmon in large pieces and fold in, or leave the fillets whole.

To pack: Divide the salad between two lunchboxes and top with arugula. Pack the dressing separately.

TRY THIS...

· Swap the salmon for 2 smoked trout or mackerel fillets, flaked (these don't need to be cooked).

· Sprinkle over some crumbled feta.

· Stir 1 tablespoon Green Pesto *(see page 154)* into the dressing.

SPICED CAULIFLOWER WITH PISTACHIOS + MINT

INGREDIENTS:

1 small cauliflower *(see note 1, page 88)*
2 skinless boneless chicken breasts
1 small piece fresh ginger
coconut oil
2 teaspoons ground turmeric/cumin
   (or a mix of the two)
1½ tablespoons honey
⅓ cup unsalted pistachios, crushed
fresh mint leaves
lemon juice

METHOD:

Boil a small amount of water (about 1 inch) in
a saucepan. Remove the thick core and outer
leaves from the cauliflower. Chop the cauliflower
into small florets and the stalks into similar-sized
chunks. Place in the pan and add a pinch of salt.
Boil for 3 minutes. Drain well.

Slice the chicken into thin strips. Peel the ginger
and grate into a frying pan. Add a little coconut
oil and the turmeric along with the cauliflower
and fry over a medium heat for 3–5 minutes until
starting to crisp up. Add the chicken and cook,
stirring regularly, for another 5–7 minutes until
cooked through.

Remove from the heat and stir through the
honey followed by the pistachios, torn mint
leaves and lemon juice to taste. Season.

To pack: Divide between the lunchboxes.

TRY THIS…

· Crumble feta on top.

· Omit the chicken and serve with roast leg
  of lamb for dinner.

TIP: Gently tear mint or basil leaves instead of chopping as they brown easily when cut.

4 IDEAS FOR CAULI RICE

Green pesto and chicken (facing page, top left)

2 skinless boneless chicken breasts
vegetable oil
²/₃ cup frozen peas
1 small cauliflower *(see note 1, page 88)*
2 portions of Green Pesto *(see page 154)*
1½ cups baby spinach leaves
lemon juice/olive oil
freshly grated Parmesan (optional)

Chop the chicken into thin strips and place in
a large frying pan with a little oil and seasoning.
Fry over medium heat for 5–7 minutes, stirring
frequently, until cooked through and slightly
browned. Remove from the pan.

While the chicken is cooking, thaw the peas in
a bowl of cold water for 1–2 minutes; drain.

Remove the thick core and outer leaves from
the cauliflower. Chop the cauliflower into
1-inch chunks, then blitz in small batches until
it resembles rice *(see note 2, page 88)*.

Place the cauli rice in the frying pan with a little
more oil and cook over medium-high heat
for 3 minutes, stirring regularly. The cauli rice
should be just cooked but still crunchy and
slightly crisp in parts. Cool.

Stir the pesto, peas, spinach and chicken through
the cauli rice. Season and add a little lemon juice
or a drizzle of olive oil to taste.

To pack: Divide between the lunchboxes and
garnish with a sprinkle of Parmesan, if you like.

Red pepper pesto (facing page, top right)

1 small cauliflower *(see note 1, page 88)*
vegetable oil
4 sun-dried tomatoes
2 jarred roasted red peppers
2 portions of Red Pepper Pesto *(see page 155)*
lemon juice
2 cups arugula

Remove the thick core and outer leaves from
the cauliflower. Chop the cauliflower into
1-inch chunks, then blitz in small batches until
it resembles rice *(see note 2, page 88)*.

Place in a frying pan with a little oil and cook
over medium-high heat for 3 minutes, stirring
regularly, until the cauli rice is just cooked through
but still crunchy and slightly crisp. Cool.

Finely slice the sun-dried tomatoes and red
peppers. Mix with the cauli rice and pesto.
Season and add a little olive oil and lemon juice
to taste.

To pack: Divide between the lunchboxes and top
with the arugula.

Nutty Mushroom

1 small cauliflower *(see note 1, page 88)*
vegetable oil
1 teaspoon ground coriander
¼ cup hazelnuts
2 garlic cloves
8 oz. button or mixed mushrooms
1 tablespoon finely chopped fresh thyme
2 oz. Parmesan
2 cups arugula
4 fresh figs (dried figs work well too)

Remove the thick core and outer leaves from
the cauliflower. Chop the cauliflower into
1-inch chunks, then blitz in small batches until
it resembles rice *(see note 2, page 88)*. Place the
cauli rice in a frying pan with a little oil and cook
over medium-high heat for 3 minutes, stirring
regularly. The cauli rice should be just cooked
but still crunchy and slightly crisp in parts. Tip
into a bowl and set aside.

Wipe the pan dry, then lightly toast the coriander
and hazelnuts in the pan over a medium heat for
2 minutes, stirring constantly. Tip into a small
bowl and set aside.

Peel and finely chop the garlic. Place in the
frying pan with a splash more oil and cook
over medium heat for 1 minute. Finely dice
three-quarters of the mushrooms and cut the
remaining mushrooms in half. Add them all to
the pan along with the coriander and hazelnuts
and the thyme. Cook over medium-high heat for
2 minutes, stirring regularly.

Add the cauli rice to the pan and mix through.
Grate over the Parmesan. Cook everything
together for a final 2–4 minutes, stirring. Season.

To pack: Divide between the lunchboxes. Pile the
arugula on top along with the quartered figs.

TRY THIS...

Oven-roast the quartered figs with a drizzle
of honey.

Kale and walnut pesto with salmon

2½ cups chopped kale
1 small cauliflower *(see note 1, page 88)*
vegetable oil
2 portions of Kale and Walnut Pesto
  (see page 155)
lemon juice
2 salmon fillets, 4–6 oz. each
⅓ cup walnut halves

Place the kale in a bowl and cover with boiling water. Leave for 5 minutes, then drain and rinse under cold water. Set aside.

Remove the thick core and outer leaves from the cauliflower. Chop the cauliflower into 1-inch chunks, then blitz in small batches until it resembles rice *(see note 2, page 88)*.

Place in a frying pan with a little oil and cook over medium-high heat for 3 minutes, stirring regularly, until the cauli rice is just cooked through but still crunchy and slightly crisp in parts. Tip into a bowl.

Stir the pesto and kale into the cauli rice. Season and add oil and lemon juice to taste.

Wipe the pan clean and heat a little more oil. Remove the skin from the salmon and cut into small chunks. Fry over medium heat for 2 minutes until just cooked. Add to the cauli rice.

Crush the walnuts (or leave them whole) and toast in the frying pan for 2 minutes until lightly golden. Mix into the salad.

To pack: Divide between the lunchboxes.

TRY THIS...

Swap the cauli rice for 1½ cups cooked quinoa, pasta or brown rice.

CAULIFLOWER, HARISSA + ALMOND SOUP

INGREDIENTS:

1 red onion
vegetable oil
¼ teaspoon ground cinnamon
½ teaspoon ground cumin
1 small cauliflower *(see note 1, page 88)*
1 garlic clove
1 cup toasted sliced almonds, plus optional extra
  to garnish
2 cups vegetable, beef or chicken stock
4–6 teaspoons harissa paste

TRY THIS...

· Add drained canned butter beans/cooked diced chicken after blitzing, and finish with crumbled feta and chopped parsley.

· Top with a dollop of Greek yogurt or sour cream.

METHOD:

Peel and finely slice the onion. Fry with a little oil in a medium-sized pan over low heat for 10 minutes until completely soft. Turn up the heat, add the spices and fry for another 2 minutes until very fragrant.

While the onion is softening, remove the outer leaves from the cauliflower and roughly chop (including the base) into small pieces. Add to the pan and cook, stirring regularly, for 5 minutes until browned. You may need to add a little more oil.

Peel and crush the garlic, then add to the pan along with the almonds. Fry for 2 more minutes. Pour in the stock—if it doesn't cover the vegetables completely, add some boiling water. Bring to a boil, then simmer for 10 minutes until the cauliflower is very tender. Stir in the harissa (to taste) and cool.

Blitz in a food processor until smooth, diluting with extra water, if needed, to reach a soup consistency. Season to taste. You may want to add a little more harissa or a squeeze of lemon juice at the end.

To pack: Split the soup between two leakproof containers. Pack extra sliced almonds separately if you want to garnish the soup. Serve warm.

TIP: Make a double batch and freeze half in individual portions.

CABBAGE

RED CABBAGE, APPLE + TAHINI SLAW
WITH SALMON + BEETS

INGREDIENTS:

2 salmon fillets, 4–6 oz. each
vegetable oil
¼ cup sesame seeds
2 apples
1 lemon
½ red cabbage
1 tablespoon chopped fresh cilantro
1½ tablespoons tahini
4 cooked and peeled beets

METHOD:

Preheat the oven to 400°F. Place the salmon on a baking sheet. Drizzle over a little oil and season with salt and pepper. Bake for 12 minutes until cooked through. After 5 minutes, sprinkle the sesame seeds onto the baking sheet alongside the salmon so they can lightly toast. Allow to cool.

While the salmon is baking, quarter the apples and remove the cores, then grate into a sieve. Press out any excess liquid. Tip the apple into a medium-sized bowl. Zest the lemon onto the apple and squeeze in the juice. Toss well.

Remove the hard outer leaves and core from the cabbage. Grate or finely slice the cabbage. Add to the apple along with the cilantro, tahini and a drizzle of oil. Mix well and season.

Slice the beets into quarters.

To pack: Spread the slaw in the lunchboxes. Place the salmon on top to one side and sprinkle with the toasted sesame seeds. Place the beets on the other side.

TRY THIS…

· Add a dollop of Greek yogurt for a creamier slaw.

· Swap the apples for carrots.

FENNEL, ORANGE, CHICKEN + HAZELNUT CABBAGE SLAW

INGREDIENTS:

2 skinless boneless chicken breasts
vegetable oil
1 fennel bulb
½ red cabbage
2 oranges
1 tablespoon honey
1 tablespoon finely chopped fresh parsley/chives
⅓ cup hazelnuts

TRY THIS...

· Add a 15.5-oz. can of chickpeas, drained and rinsed, for extra protein, or instead of the chicken.

· Swap the orange for grapefruit, or peach pieces with added lemon juice.

· Sprinkle with crumbled feta.

METHOD:

Preheat the oven to 400°F. Place the chicken on a baking sheet and drizzle over a little oil. Season. Bake for 18–20 minutes until cooked through. Cool, then thinly slice (or leave whole).

While the chicken is cooking, remove the hard outer pieces/leaves from the fennel and cabbage. Cut out the cabbage core. Finely shred the fennel and cabbage with a knife and place in a bowl.

Cut one orange in half and squeeze the juice over the fennel and cabbage. Peel the other orange and separate into segments. Add to the bowl along with the chicken, honey, herbs and a drizzle of oil. Mix well and season to taste.

To pack: Spoon into the lunchboxes. Coarsely crush the nuts and sprinkle on top.

TOFU PAD THAI

INGREDIENTS:

3–4 oz. tofu
½ cup soy sauce
½ red cabbage
lemon juice
4 carrots
6 oz. sugarsnap peas
5 oz. glass noodles
2 tablespoons honey (optional)
2 tablespoons chopped fresh cilantro
¼ cup toasted sesame seeds/unsalted peanuts

TRY THIS...

· Pickle the red cabbage—half an hour ahead, marinate it in 4 tablespoons each white wine vinegar, vegetable oil and honey, then drain.

· Sprinkle over some cooked shrimp at the end.

· Instead of dressing the noodles with the reduced soy sauce, use our Peanut Teriyaki Sauce (*see page 156*).

METHOD:

Preheat the oven to 350°F.

Cut the tofu into 1-inch cubes. Place in a bowl with the soy sauce—the tofu cubes should be covered. Leave to marinate for 10 minutes.

Meanwhile, remove the coarse outer leaves and core from the red cabbage. Grate and place in a bowl. Toss with a squeeze of lemon juice to keep fresh. Peel and spiralize the carrots.

Slice the sugarsnap peas in half lengthways, on the diagonal. Cover with boiling water and leave for 2 minutes. Drain and immediately tip into a bowl of cold water, then drain again. Set aside.

Bring a medium pot of water to a boil. Add the glass noodles and simmer for 3–5 minutes until just cooked. Drain and rinse under cold water. Place in a bowl and snip up roughly with scissors (smaller pieces will be easier to eat at your desk).

While the noodles are cooking, drain the soy sauce from the tofu into a pan and reduce over low heat until sticky. Cool, then toss into the noodles. Sweeten with honey, if you like.

Line a baking sheet with parchment paper and lay out the marinated tofu cubes. Bake for 10 minutes until golden, turning the tofu halfway through. Cool.

Mix the cilantro through the noodles, along with the sesame seeds or peanuts.

To pack: Place the noodles, carrots, cabbage and sugarsnaps in separate sections in the lunchboxes and dot the tofu on top.

CABBAGE CARAWAY CHICKEN SALAD

INGREDIENTS:

2 skinless boneless chicken breasts
4 tablespoons finely chopped fresh parsley
2 tablespoons vegetable oil
½ red cabbage
¼ white cabbage
2 teaspoons caraway seeds
1 lemon
2 tablespoons Dijon mustard
1 tablespoon cider vinegar
2½ cups arugula

TRY THIS...

Add some cucumber moons for extra crunch—cut cucumber in half lengthways and scoop out the seeds with a spoon, then slice across to create thin moons.

METHOD:

Preheat the oven to 400°F. Place the chicken on a baking sheet. Mix the parsley with the oil to form a green paste. Spread over the chicken and season with salt and pepper. Bake for 18–20 minutes until just cooked. Allow to cool, then slice at an angle.

While the chicken is in the oven, remove the tough outer leaves and core from the cabbages. Grate and place in a bowl.

Lightly toast the caraway seeds in a small dry pan over medium heat for 3 minutes. Zest the lemon. Add to the cabbage along with the caraway seeds, mustard, vinegar and some lemon juice, if you like. Toss together well.

To pack: Spoon the cabbage into the lunchboxes and add the chicken. Pile the arugula on top.

CHICKEN AIOLI SALAD

INGREDIENTS:

2 skinless boneless chicken breasts

2 lemons

4 tablespoons mixed seeds

vegetable oil

¾ cup long grain and wild rice blend

⅔ cup frozen peas

½ red or white cabbage (or mix of ¼ red
and ¼ white, which is prettier)

1 garlic clove

4 tablespoons Greek yogurt

METHOD:

Preheat the oven to 400°F. Place the chicken on a baking sheet. Zest the lemons and sprinkle over the chicken along with the mixed seeds, a drizzle of oil and a pinch of salt. Bake for 18–20 minutes. Allow to cool, then slice at an angle.

While the chicken is in the oven, put the rice in a pan with 1½ cups of water and a pinch of salt. Cover and bring to a boil, then reduce heat and simmer for 25 minutes or according to package directions until al dente. Drain. Place in a bowl, season with salt and pepper and stir in the peas.

Remove the tough outer leaves and core from the cabbage, then finely slice.

To make the dressing, peel and finely chop the garlic, then mix with the yogurt, the juice from one lemon and a pinch of salt.

To pack: Spoon the rice into one half of each lunchbox and the cabbage in the other. Fan the sliced chicken across the rice. Tuck in a wedge of lemon. Pack the dressing separately.

PEAR, BACON, CABBAGE + ARUGULA SALAD

INGREDIENTS:

2 pears
4 strips of bacon
½ cup walnuts/pecans (sliced almonds also
    work well)
2 tablespoons honey
½ white cabbage
2 teaspoons Dijon or whole grain mustard
    (or lemon juice to taste)
2 tablespoons cider vinegar
2 tablespoons vegetable oil
1½ cups arugula

METHOD:

Preheat the oven to 400°F. Peel the pears and slice into quarters lengthways. Remove the core, then slice each quarter in half lengthways so you have 16 pieces in all. Place on a baking sheet.

Cut the bacon strips across into smaller pieces and pile on another baking sheet. Crush the nuts and mix with the bacon along with the honey. Spread out the bacon in a single layer. Bake both trays for 10–12 minutes, stirring every few minutes, until the bacon is cooked. The pear should still be quite firm. Allow to cool.

Meanwhile, remove the tough outer cabbage leaves and the core, then grate the cabbage. Whisk the mustard with the vinegar and oil, then thoroughly mix through the cabbage.

Add the pears and bacon and season with salt and pepper.

To pack: Spoon the salad into the lunchboxes and top with the arugula.

TRY THIS…

· Scatter crumbled blue or goat cheese on top before the arugula, or add a dollop of crème fraîche.

· Serve the baked pears and bacon on sourdough toast with Greek yogurt for brunch.

3 IDEAS FOR ZUCCHINI NOODLE JARS

Thai green pot

¾ cup frozen shelled edamame beans

3 zucchini

4 oz. green beans

1½ cups chopped kale

4 oz. sugarsnap peas

1–4 teaspoons Thai green curry paste (add more or less depending on how spicy you want it)

Thaw the edamame in a bowl of cold water for 1–2 minutes, then drain. Meanwhile, trim the zucchini, then spiralize into long, thin strands (alternatively, shave into ribbons with a peeler, discarding the watery center). Trim the green beans and slice into short pieces.

To pack: Split all the ingredients between the lunchboxes (or heatproof jars). Before eating, add 1 cup boiling water to the ingredients. Stir and leave for 2–3 minutes before eating.

TRY THIS…

Garnish with a handful of toasted sliced almonds, packed separately.

Tofu pho

4 zucchini

3–4 oz. tofu

1 small piece fresh ginger

2 spring onions or scallions (white bulbs and most of the green)

1 cup bean sprouts

15 fresh mint leaves

2 vegetable bouillon cubes

soy sauce/sweet chilli sauce (optional)

lime wedges

Trim the zucchini, then spiralize into long, thin strands (alternatively, shave into ribbons with a peeler, discarding the watery center). Cut the tofu into cubes. Peel and finely dice the ginger. Slice the spring onions.

To pack: Split all the prepared ingredients between the lunchboxes (or heatproof jars). Add the bean sprouts, mint and crumbled bouillon cube. Before serving, add 1 cup boiling water to the ingredients. Stir and leave for 2–3 minutes. Season with a little soy sauce or sweet chilli sauce, if you like, and lime juice to taste (pack the wedges separately).

Rainbow pot

¾ cup frozen shelled edamame beans
3 zucchini
2 carrots
1 small piece fresh ginger
2 spring onions (white bulbs only)
2 vegetable bouillon cubes
2 cups chopped kale
2 handfuls bean sprouts
1 tablespoon chopped fresh cilantro
soy sauce or sweet chilli sauce (optional)

Thaw the edamame in a bowl of cold water for 1–2 minutes; drain. Meanwhile, trim the zucchini, then spiralize into long, thin strands (alternatively, shave into ribbons with a peeler, discarding the watery center). Peel and spiralize the carrots. Peel and grate the ginger. Finely slice the spring onion bulbs.

To pack: Crumble a bouillon cube into each lunchbox (or heatproof jar). Add the prepared ingredients along with the kale, bean sprouts, cilantro and edamame beans. Before eating, add 1 cup boiling water to the ingredients. Stir and leave for 2–3 minutes. Season with a little soy sauce or sweet chilli sauce, if you like.

TRY THIS…

· Add leftover roast chicken, cut into small pieces, or a few squares of tofu.

· Spice up the noodle jar by adding a teaspoon of curry paste (tikka, green or red all work well).

ZUCCHINI NOODLES + RED PEPPER PESTO

INGREDIENTS:

3 zucchini
1 fresh red chili pepper
1 red pepper
1 x 15.5-oz. can butter beans
1/4 cup unsalted cashews
1 mozzarella ball (or a handful of mini ones)
light olive oil
2 portions of Red Pepper Pesto *(see page 155)*
2 cups arugula

TRY THIS...

Add mini turkey meatballs—mix together
8 oz. ground turkey, 2 teaspoons garlic powder,
1 tablespoon finely chopped fresh parsley and
the zest of 1/2 lemon. Season with salt and
pepper. Roll into small tablespoon-sized balls.
Place on a baking sheet and bake in a preheated
350°F oven for 15–20 minutes or until cooked
through.

METHOD:

Trim the zucchini, then spiralize into long, thin
strands (alternatively, shave into ribbons with a
peeler, discarding the watery center.)

Cut the chili pepper in half lengthways and
remove the seeds using a teaspoon, then finely
dice. Remove the core and seeds from the red
pepper, then slice into thin strips.

Drain and rinse the butter beans. Place in a bowl
and mix through the chili pepper (to taste), red
pepper, cashews, torn mozzarella and a splash of
oil. Season.

To pack: Pile the zucchini noodles in one side of
the lunchboxes and top with a dollop of pesto.
Spoon the bean salad on the other side of
the lunchboxes and top with arugula.

ZUCCHINI NOODLES WITH KALE + WALNUT PESTO-BAKED SALMON

INGREDIENTS:

2 salmon fillets, 4-6 oz. each
2 portions of Kale and Walnut Pesto
  (see page 155)
2 handfuls of cherry tomatoes
vegetable oil
3 zucchini
2½ cups watercress

TRY THIS...

Spiralize beets or butternut squash instead
of zucchini, toss with a little oil and bake in
a 350°F oven for 10 minutes.

METHOD:

Preheat the oven to 400°F. Line a baking sheet
with parchment paper. Place the salmon on one
side of the tray. Spread the pesto across the top
of the salmon, ensuring the fillets are completely
covered. Bake for 12 minutes until cooked
through. Halfway through cooking, scatter the
cherry tomatoes on the other side of the tray,
drizzle them with a little oil and sprinkle with salt.

Meanwhile, trim the zucchini, then spiralize into
noodles (alternatively, shave into ribbons with a
peeler, discarding the watery center).

To pack: Spread the zucchini noodles in the
lunchboxes. Once the salmon and tomatoes have
cooled, flake the salmon and scatter over the top
with the tomatoes and watercress.

RIBBONED ZUCCHINI SALAD WITH THAI FISHCAKES

INGREDIENTS:

Fishcakes
1 large peeled sweet potato
4 oz. green beans
2 skinless salmon fillets, 4-6 oz. each
2 tablespoons Thai green curry paste
⅓ cup dried shredded coconut

Salad
12 asparagus spears
3 zucchini
juice of 1 lemon

TRY THIS…

· Serve with sweet chilli sauce or crème fraîche.

· Swap the salmon for mackerel or cod fillet.

METHOD:

Preheat the oven to 400°F.

Make the fishcakes first. Cut the sweet potato into small chunks. Place in a pan with a pinch of salt, cover with water and bring to a boil, then cook for 6–8 minutes until just soft. Drain. Mash until smooth with a potato masher or fork.

While the sweet potato is cooking, trim the green beans and cut into very short pieces. Place in a bowl, cover with boiling water and leave for 4 minutes, then drain. Slice the asparagus spears for the salad in half lengthways and place in another bowl. Cover with boiling water and leave for 3 minutes, then drain.

Dice the salmon and place in a blender with the curry paste. Blitz until smooth. Mix through the mashed sweet potato and season with salt and pepper. Add the green beans. Shape the mix into 4–6 balls and press each down to form an oval cake. Dip both sides in shredded coconut to coat. Place the coated fishcakes on a baking sheet lined with parchment paper and bake for 12–15 minutes, turning over halfway through, until golden brown.

Meanwhile, make the salad. Trim the zucchini, then shave into ribbons using a vegetable peeler. Toss with the asparagus, lemon juice and a little salt.

To pack: Split the salad between the lunchboxes. Once the fishcakes are cool, lay them on top of the salad.

ZUCCHINI NOODLE + SWEET POTATO SALAD WITH AVOCADO DRESSING

INGREDIENTS:

2 sweet potatoes
3 zucchini
⅓ cup unsalted cashews
2 handfuls of pomegranate seeds
10 fresh basil leaves

Dressing
¼ avocado
¼ cup unsalted cashews
2 teaspoons cider vinegar
1 tablespoon light olive oil

METHOD:

Peel the sweet potatoes and cut into small cubes. Place in a pan, cover with water and add a pinch of salt. Bring to a boil and cook for 6–8 minutes until cooked through. Drain and rinse in cold water to cool quickly.

While the sweet potatoes are cooking, trim the zucchini, then spiralize into thin strands (alternatively, shave into ribbons with a peeler, discarding the watery center). Toast the cashews for the salad in a dry pan over medium heat for 2 minutes until lightly golden.

Blitz all the ingredients for the dressing together in a food processor or blender. Season with salt and pepper to taste and loosen with a little water, if necessary.

To pack: Divide the zucchini noodles and sweet potato between the lunchboxes and sprinkle with the pomegranate seeds, torn basil and toasted cashews. Pack the dressing separately.

TRY THIS…

· Add 1 teaspoon harissa paste or tahini to the dressing, or a handful of chopped fresh herbs (basil/parsley/cilantro).

· Make the dressing a dip by adding a dollop of natural yogurt, extra cashews and avocado.

GREEN PESTO-BAKED SALMON WITH CUCUMBER + ZUCCHINI RIBBONS

INGREDIENTS:

2 salmon fillets, 4–6 oz. each
2 portions of Green Pesto *(see page 154)*
2 zucchini
1 cucumber
light olive oil
2 teaspoons snipped fresh dill (or chives)
2½ cups arugula (or mixed greens)
2 tablespoons mixed seeds (optional)

METHOD:

Preheat the oven to 400°F. Place the salmon on a baking sheet. Spread the pesto across the top of each fillet, then bake for 12 minutes. Remove and cool.

Meanwhile, trim the zucchini and cucumber. Use a peeler to shave them both into ribbons, discarding the inner watery part. Place the ribbons in a bowl. Add a light splash of oil, the chopped dill and some salt and toss together.

To pack: Pile the zucchini and cucumber ribbons in one half of the lunchboxes and the arugula in the other half. Lay the salmon diagonally across the arugula and ribbons. Sprinkle over the mixed seeds.

TRY THIS…

Swap the salmon for tofu and broccolini. Cut 8 oz. tofu into cubes and 6 stems of broccolini into similar-sized chunks. Mix with the pesto and bake in a 350°F oven for 15–18 minutes until the broccolini is al dente.

GREEN
BEANS

CRUNCHY OAT-SESAME CHICKEN + GREEN BEAN SALAD

INGREDIENTS:

8 oz. green beans
2 skinless boneless chicken breasts
vegetable oil
¼ cup old fashioned oats
3 tablespoons sesame seeds
2 teaspoons dried Italian herbs
1 tablespoon honey
2 teaspoons toasted sesame oil
2 cups arugula

METHOD:

Bring a pot of water to a gentle boil. Trim the green beans, then place in the pot with a pinch of salt. Cook for 3–4 minutes until al dente. Drain and rinse under cold water.

Cut the chicken into small strips. Place in a pan with a splash of oil. Cook over medium-high heat, stirring regularly, for 5–7 minutes until golden and cooked through. Remove from the pan.

Add a little more oil to the pan along with the oats, sesame seeds and Italian herbs. Fry over a medium heat, stirring, for 3–5 minutes until golden brown. Remove from the heat and stir in the honey, sesame oil, green beans and chicken.

To pack: Cool, then spoon the salad into the lunchboxes and top with the arugula.

TRY THIS…

· Add a handful of sweet potato wedges roasted with a little oil in a 400°F oven for 30 minutes, tossed every 10 minutes.

· Swap the sesame seeds or oats for dried shredded coconut.

GOAT CHEESE-STUFFED FIGS

INGREDIENTS:

4 fresh figs
2–3 oz. goat cheese
4 slices prosciutto
2 tablespoons olive oil, plus extra for drizzling
½ cup walnuts
1 tablespoon honey, plus extra for drizzling
8 oz. green beans
2 cups mixed greens
1 tablespoon balsamic vinegar (or 2 teaspoons
   whole grain/Dijon mustard)

TRY THIS…

· Swap the goat cheese for mascarpone/cream
  cheese/feta.

· If figs aren't in season, you can use pears.
  Or simply sprinkle crumbled goat cheese
  and strips of prosciutto over the beans and
  leaves and add 4 sliced dried figs or apricots.

· Switch to a quick blue cheese dressing. Gently
  melt 2 oz. blue cheese in a pan with a splash
  of milk/cream and olive oil. Season and add
  lemon juice to taste. Cool before packing.

METHOD:

Preheat the oven to 350°F.

Place the figs on a baking sheet and cut a cross
on the top of each to open it up slightly. Split
the goat cheese among the figs, squashing it
into the center. Wrap each fig with a slice of
prosciutto. Drizzle with oil and season with salt
and pepper.

Bake for 12–15 minutes until the figs are slightly
oozing and the prosciutto is crisp. About 3
minutes before the figs have finished cooking,
add the nuts to the tray and drizzle with a little
honey.

While the figs are in the oven, trim the green
beans and cut in half. Bring a pot of water to
a gentle boil. Add the green beans and a pinch
of salt. Boil for 4 minutes until al dente. Drain
and rinse under cold water (this will keep them
green and prevent further cooking). Mix with
the greens.

Whisk together the 2 tablespoons olive oil,
1 tablespoon honey and vinegar to make a
dressing. Season to taste with salt and pepper.

To pack: Spread the mixed greens and green
beans on the bottom of the lunchboxes and
set the cooled figs and honeyed walnuts on top.
Pack the dressing separately.

COCONUT CHICKEN + TAMARIND SALAD

INGREDIENTS:

2 skinless boneless chicken breasts
8 oz. green beans
4 oz. sugarsnap peas (or frozen shelled
   edamame beans)
⅔ cup frozen peas
20 fresh basil leaves
¼ cup dried shredded coconut

Tamarind dressing
1 tablespoon vegetable oil,
   plus extra for drizzling
2 tablespoons tamarind paste
juice of 1 lime

METHOD:

Preheat the oven to 400°F. Place the chicken on a baking sheet, drizzle with a little oil and season. Bake for 18–20 minutes until cooked through. Allow to cool, then slice into strips.

While the chicken is in the oven, trim the green beans and bring a pot of water to a boil. Add the beans with a pinch of salt. Cook for 5 minutes until al dente. Drain and rinse under cold water.

Put the sugarsnap peas in a bowl and cover with boiling water. Leave for 2 minutes, then drain and rinse under cold water. Thaw the frozen peas (and edamame, if using), in a bowl of cold water for 1–2 minutes; drain. Mix the sugarsnaps and peas with the green beans and torn basil.

Toast the coconut in a dry pan over medium heat until golden brown.

Whisk the dressing ingredients together with 1 tablespoon water and seasoning to taste.

To pack: Spoon the salad into the lunchboxes, top with the chicken slices and sprinkle the toasted coconut on top. Pack the dressing separately.

TRY THIS…

· Add a sliced fresh red chili pepper for some heat.

· Toast a bigger batch of coconut and use the rest as a breakfast topper stirred through Greek yogurt or mixed through granola.

PEANUT TERIYAKI GREEN BEANS + TOFU

INGREDIENTS:

½ cup long grain and wild rice blend

8 oz. tofu

2 teaspoons cornstarch

3 tablespoons toasted sesame oil (or vegetable oil)

8 oz. green beans

¾ cup frozen shelled edamame beans

2 portions of Peanut Teriyaki Sauce *(see page 156)*

TRY THIS...

Swap the tofu for salmon. Double the teriyaki sauce and spoon half over 2 salmon fillets, then bake in a 400°F oven for 12 minutes until just cooked through. Flake through the salad.

METHOD:

Preheat the oven to 350°F. Put the rice in a pan with 1 cup of water and a pinch of salt. Boil for 15–18 minutes or according to package directions until al dente. Drain.

While the rice is cooking, briefly drain the tofu on paper towel, then cut into 1-inch cubes. Put the tofu in a bowl with the cornstarch and sesame oil. Gently toss together, ensuring the tofu cubes are completely covered by the cornstarch. Spread out on a baking sheet lined with parchment paper and bake for 15 minutes until golden brown. Flip the tofu cubes over halfway through cooking.

Boil a pot of water. Trim the green beans, then place in the pot and add a pinch of salt. Cook for 5 minutes, then drain and rinse under cold water.

Thaw the edamame beans in a bowl of cold water for 1–2 minutes; drain.

To pack: Spoon the vegetables and rice into the lunchboxes and sprinkle the tofu on top. Pack the sauce separately. To eat, mix the sauce through the tofu: the cornstarch will absorb the flavors.

THAI BAKED HALLOUMI SALAD

INGREDIENTS:

4–6 oz. halloumi cheese (or tofu/feta)
2 teaspoons Thai green curry paste
juice of ½ lemon
½ cup unsalted cashews
¾ cup green beans
4 spring onions or scallions (white bulbs and
    most of the green)
2½ cups baby spinach leaves

Dressing
1–2 teaspoons Thai green curry paste
juice of ½ lemon
2 teaspoons honey
2 tablespoons olive oil

TRY THIS…

· Fry 2 handfuls of raw peeled shrimp or prawns
  in a teaspoon of Thai green curry paste until
  pink. Cool, then add to the bean salad.

· Add 2 handfuls of pomegranate seeds/dried
  cranberries and a chopped avocado dressed
  with lime juice.

METHOD:

Preheat the oven to 400°F. Slice the halloumi
into thin strips and place on a sheet of foil on a
baking sheet. Spread with the curry paste and
lemon juice, then wrap into a packet. Cook in
the oven for 5 minutes.

Add the cashews to the baking sheet alongside
the foil packet and cook for another 5 minutes
until golden brown. Cool.

While the cheese is in the oven, trim the green
beans and bring a pot of water to a boil. Add the
beans with a pinch of salt. Cook for 4 minutes
until al dente. Drain and rinse under cold water.
Finely slice the spring onions.

Whisk the ingredients for the dressing together,
adding curry paste to taste (depending on how
spicy you like it).

To pack: Spread the green beans in the
lunchboxes and lay the halloumi on top followed
by the spring onions, spinach and nuts. Pack the
dressing separately.

MEXICAN GREEN BEANS

INGREDIENTS:

8 oz. green beans
²/₃ cup frozen shelled edamame beans
1 x 15.5-oz. can kidney beans
1 tablespoon cumin seeds
1 x 8.5-oz. can sweet corn kernels
vegetable oil
2 red peppers
4 spring onions or scallions (white bulbs and most
   of the green)
1 tablespoon chopped fresh cilantro (optional)

TRY THIS…

· Add some leftover cooked chicken—shred with
two forks, then toss with a little olive oil, salt
and chopped fresh cilanto. Toast 2 teaspoons
smoked paprika or ground cumin in a dry pan
for 3 minutes, then stir through.

· Mix in 1 cup cooked quinoa or bulgur wheat.

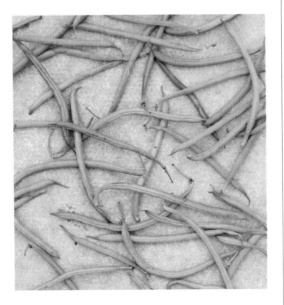

METHOD:

Boil a pot of water. Trim the green beans and
cut into quarters. Place in the pot with a pinch
of salt. Cook for 5 minutes, then drain and rinse
under cold water. Tip into a bowl.

Thaw the edamame beans in a bowl of cold
water for 1–2 minutes; drain. Drain and rinse the
kidney beans. Add both beans to the green beans
in the bowl.

Grind the cumin seeds to a powder in a mortar
and pestle (or use ground cumin). Drain and
rinse the corn. Place in a pan with a splash of
oil, the cumin and a pinch of salt. Cook over
medium-high heat, stirring, for 2–3 minutes until
the corn begins to darken and the cumin is very
fragrant. Cool.

Remove the core and seeds from the red peppers,
then slice into ½-inch-thick strips. Finely slice the
spring onions. Add the peppers, corn and spring
onions to the bowl of beans and toss well to mix.
Add a little oil and season with salt and pepper.

To pack: Spoon the salad into the lunchboxes and
sprinkle the cilantro on top.

GREEN BEAN MINESTRONE

INGREDIENTS:

1 leek
1 garlic clove (optional)
vegetable oil
2 carrots
2 cups chopped kale
2 teaspoons smoked paprika
1 vegetable bouillon cube
½ cup orzo pasta
2 tablespoons fresh basil, torn
8 oz. green beans

TRY THIS…

· Add a handful of grated Parmesan before packing the soup.

· Swap the pasta for rice.

METHOD:

Finely slice the leek. Peel and finely chop the garlic (if using). Place both in a pan with a little oil and a pinch of salt. Cook over medium heat for 3 minutes until soft, stirring regularly.

Meanwhile, peel the carrots and dice into small pieces. Add to the pan and cook for another 3 minutes.

Add the kale along with the smoked paprika, crumbled bouillon cube, pasta and basil. Pour in 4 cups water. Trim the green beans and cut in half, then add to the pan. Bring to a boil and simmer for about 8 minutes until the pasta is al dente. Season.

To pack: Allow the minestrone to cool before packing in leakproof containers. Reheat to serve.

BROCCOLI

BROCCOLINI + RED PESTO LENTILS

INGREDIENTS:

¾ cup green lentils
8 oz. broccolini
10 cherry tomatoes
2 jarred roasted red peppers
olive oil
lemon (optional)
10 fresh basil leaves
2 oz. goat cheese/toasted pine nuts (optional)
2 portions of Red Pepper Pesto *(see page 155)*

METHOD:

Put the lentils in a pan, add 1½ cups water and a pinch of salt and bring to a simmer over medium-high heat. Cook for 15–20 minutes until al dente. Drain.

While the lentils are cooking, trim the ends from the broccolini and slice the stems in half on an angle, then boil another pot of water. Add broccolini with a pinch of salt, then cook for 4–5 minutes until al dente. Drain and rinse under cold water.

Cut the cherry tomatoes in half. Cut the red peppers into thin strips.

Put the lentils in a bowl and dress with a little olive oil and season with salt and pepper plus lemon zest/juice, if you like.

To pack: When the lentils and broccolini are cool, spread the lentils in the lunchboxes. Arrange everything else on top in sections, then sprinkle with torn basil and goat cheese/pine nuts, if using. Pack the pesto separately. Alternatively, mix everything together before packing.

TRY THIS…

Double the pesto and mix half of it through 2 chopped skinless boneless chicken breasts, then bake these in a 400°F oven for 13–15 minutes until cooked through. Sprinkle the chicken over the lentils and vegetables.

MUSHROOM + PEA PASTA WITH BROCCOLI SAUCE

INGREDIENTS:

2 cups shell pasta (conchiglie)
1 medium head of broccoli
2 garlic cloves
4 oz. button or mixed mushrooms
vegetable oil
$\frac{1}{2}$ cup frozen peas
$\frac{1}{3}$ cup crème fraîche
1 tablespoon finely chopped fresh parsley
1 lemon

METHOD:

Boil a large pot of water. Add the pasta with a pinch of salt and cook 12–14 minutes or according to package directions until al dente. Drain, reserving $\frac{1}{2}$ cup of the pasta water.

While the pasta is cooking, boil another pot of water. Cut off the broccoli florets and cut the stalk into similar-sized pieces. Put the stalk pieces in the pot with a pinch of salt. Cook for 1 minute, then add the florets and cook for another 2–3 minutes until al dente. Drain and rinse under cold water.

Peel and finely chop the garlic. Quarter the mushrooms. Put the garlic in a pan with a splash of oil and fry over a low heat for 2 minutes. Add half the broccoli, the mushrooms and peas. Cook over a high heat for 5 minutes, stirring frequently. Remove from the heat.

Combine the crème fraîche, reserved pasta water, parsley and remaining broccoli in a food processor. Blitz until smooth to make a thick sauce. Stir the sauce into the pasta along with the peas and mushrooms. Zest the lemon into the pasta and season to taste with the juice, salt and pepper.

To pack: Spoon into your lunchboxes.

TRY THIS… Add a cooked and flaked fillet of salmon.

SMOKY BROCCOLI + BACON SALAD

INGREDIENTS:

4 strips of smoked bacon
1/2 cup sliced almonds
1 medium head of broccoli
vegetable oil
2 teaspoons smoked paprika
2 teaspoons honey (optional)
2 red peppers
2 1/2 cups arugula
lemon wedges (optional)

TRY THIS...

· Swap the bacon for 1/2 cup crumbled feta.

· Use 2 teaspoons chipotle or harissa paste
  instead of smoked paprika.

METHOD:

Preheat the oven to 400°F. Lay the bacon on a
baking sheet and roast for 10–15 minutes until
the bacon is crisp. Add the almonds to the tray
about 5 minutes before the bacon is done. Break
up the bacon into pieces.

Meanwhile, cut off the broccoli florets and cut
the stalk into similar-sized pieces. Put in a pan
with a little oil and the smoked paprika. Season
with salt and pepper. Fry over medium heat
for 5 minutes until the broccoli is just cooked
but is still very crunchy. Remove from the heat
and drizzle over the honey, if using. Toss and
set aside.

Remove the core and seeds from the peppers,
then cut into chunks.

To pack: Once cool, place the bacon, broccoli,
peppers and rocket in sections in the lunchboxes.
Garnish with the toasted flaked almonds and
tuck in a wedge of lemon, if you like.

BROCCOLI-WALNUT "RICE" + SALMON

INGREDIENTS:

2 salmon fillets, 4–6 oz. each
1 small piece fresh ginger
vegetable oil
2 teaspoons honey
1 medium head of broccoli (or 10 stalks
   of broccolini)
½ cup walnuts
2 cups chopped kale
2 teaspoons tahini

TRY THIS…

· Sprinkle with a handful of pomegranate seeds
  or ½ cup crumbled feta.

· Tuck in a lemon wedge to squeeze over before
  eating.

METHOD:

Preheat the oven to 400°F and boil a pot of
water. Place the salmon on a lined baking sheet.
Peel the ginger and grate over the salmon. Mix
the ginger with a little oil and season with salt
and pepper. Drizzle with honey and bake for
12 minutes until just cooked.

Meanwhile, split the head of broccoli lengthways
in half (or take 5 of the broccolini stalks) and
trim the ends. Add to the pot of boiling water
with a pinch of salt. Cook for 4 minutes until
al dente. Drain and rinse under cold water.

Finely chop the rest of the broccoli. Chop the
walnuts into similar-sized pieces. Combine the
finely chopped broccoli and walnuts in a frying
pan with a little oil and seasoning, and cook over
medium heat for 3 minutes until just soft, stirring
occasionally. Set aside.

Put the kale in a bowl and cover with boiling
water. Leave for 4 minutes, then drain and rinse
under cold water. Squeeze out any excess water
before mixing the kale with the fried broccoli and
walnut "rice." Stir through the tahini and a little
more oil and season well.

To pack: Spoon the "rice" mix into the lunchboxes
and top with the broccoli pieces and whole
salmon fillets.

BROCCOLI LINGUINI WITH GREEN PESTO + PINE NUTS

INGREDIENTS:

4 oz. linguini
olive oil
1 medium head of broccoli
½–1 teaspoon crushed red pepper, to taste
3 cups baby spinach leaves
2 portions of Green Pesto *(see page 154)*
¼ cup toasted pine nuts
½ cup Parmesan shavings

METHOD:

Boil a large pot of water. Add the linguini with a good pinch of salt. Cook for 8–10 minutes or according to package directions until al dente. Drain and mix with a little olive oil to prevent sticking.

While the pasta is cooking, bring another pot of water to a boil. Cut off the broccoli florets and cut the stalk into similar-sized pieces. Put the broccoli stalk pieces in the pot with a pinch of salt. Cook for 1 minute. Add the florets and cook for a further 2–3 minutes until al dente. Drain and rinse under cold water.

Heat a large pan with a splash of olive oil over low heat. Add the crushed red pepper, spinach and broccoli, turn up the heat and fry for 3 minutes. Remove from the heat and stir in the linguini and pesto.

To pack: Once cooled, spoon the pasta salad into the lunchboxes and sprinkle the pine nuts and Parmesan on top.

TRY THIS…

· For a stripped-back lunch, try without the pesto and add extra olive oil and some lemon juice.

· Add salmon. Drizzle oil over 1–2 x 4-oz. salmon fillets and sprinkle over some dried Italian herbs or extra pesto. Bake in a 400°F oven for about 12 minutes until cooked through. Flake and stir through the pasta.

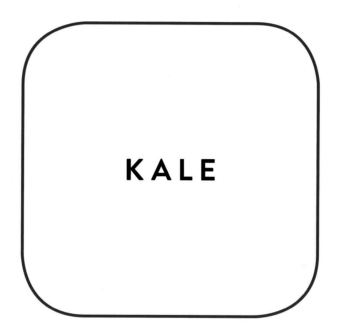

KALE

KALE PASTA SALAD WITH COCONUT-LIME DRESSING

INGREDIENTS:

1½ cups whole wheat pasta shells
4 oz. broccolini
2½ cups chopped kale
2 portions of Coconut-lime Dressing
  (see page 153)
¾ cup arugula

TRY THIS…

Drizzle a little oil over 2 trout fillets, sprinkle with some sesame seeds and bake in a 400°F oven for 10 minutes. Flake over the pasta salad in the lunchboxes before adding the arugula.

METHOD:

Boil a large pot of water. Add the pasta with a pinch of salt and boil for 12–15 minutes or according to package directions until al dente. Drain well.

While the pasta is cooking, bring another pot of water to a boil. Trim the ends off the broccolini, then cut the stems in half. Add to the pot with a pinch of salt. Boil for 4–5 minutes until al dente. Drain and rinse under cold water.

Put the kale in a bowl, cover with boiling water and leave for 4–5 minutes. Drain and rinse under cold water, then squeeeze out excess water.

Combine the pasta, kale and broccolini with the coconut dressing.

To pack: Once cool, spoon the salad into the lunchboxes and place the arugula leaves on top.

KALE, BEET + WALNUT HASH

INGREDIENTS:	METHOD:
2 sweet potatoes 1 red onion 4 cooked and peeled beets 2 garlic cloves vegetable oil 1½ cups chopped kale ½ cup walnuts *Tahini dressing* 4 tablespoons tahini juice of 1 lemon, or to taste	Peel and dice the sweet potato into small chunks. Place in a pan with a pinch of salt and cover with water. Bring to a boil and simmer for 6–8 minutes until just cooked through. Drain. While the sweet potatoes are cooking, peel the onion and chop with the beets into small chunks. Peel and finely chop the garlic. Heat a pan with a little oil and add the cooked sweet potato, beets and red onion. Fry over medium heat for 5 minutes, stirring frequently. Stir in the kale, garlic and walnuts and cook for another 5 minutes. Keep stirring. Make the dressing by mixing the tahini and lemon juice with ¼ cup water. Season with salt and pepper. *To pack:* Allow the salad to cool before dividing between two lunchboxes. Pack the dressing separately.

TRY THIS… When frying the sweet potato, beet and onion, add 2 diced sausages or chicken fillets and fry until cooked through.

3 KALE FRITTATAS

Kale, ricotta and squash frittata

½ large butternut squash
2 cups chopped kale
6 eggs
4 tablespoons ricotta
2 tablespoons mixed seeds

Salad
¾ cup chopped kale (or baby kale leaves)
1 avocado
juice of ½ lemon
½ cucumber

Preheat the oven to 350°F. Peel the squash and dice into small cubes. Place in a pan, cover with water and add a pinch of salt. Bring to a boil and cook for 5 minutes over medium heat until just cooked through. Drain.

While the squash is cooking, chop the kale, then place in a bowl and cover with boiling water. Leave for 5 minutes to soften. Drain and rinse under cold water.

Crack the eggs into a bowl, add salt to taste and whisk together with a fork. Mix through the cooked squash, ricotta and kale. Season.

Wipe a large muffin tin with oil using paper towels. Pour the egg mix into the holes to fill them three-quarters full (you can make 6–8 frittatas). Sprinkle the seeds on top. Place in the middle of the oven and bake for 10–15 minutes until each frittata is firm in the center. Using a spatula, loosen the sides gently, then flip out on to a wire rack to cool.

For the salad, place the kale in a bowl. Peel the avocado and cut into strips, then mix with the lemon juice to prevent browning. Cut the cucumber in half lengthways and remove the seeds with a teaspoon. Slice into half-moon shapes. Add the avocado and cucumber to the bowl and toss gently with the kale (or keep these three elements separate).

To pack: Place 3 or 4 frittatas on one side in each lunchbox with the salad alongside.

TRY THIS…

· Add chopped prosciutto or cooked chicken to the egg mix.

· Serve with a sweet chilli dressing: mix 1 tablespoon sweet chilli sauce with a splash of olive oil and the juice of ½ lemon. Pack separately.

TIP:

If you don't have a muffin tin, you can cook the frittata in an ovenproof frying pan or round pan, then cut into quarters to serve.

Kale, leek and goat cheese frittata

3 cups chopped kale
1 leek
6 eggs
2 teaspoons dried oregano
coconut/olive oil
2 oz. goat cheese
3 tablespoons mixed seeds
4 cherry tomatoes

Salad
¾ cup mixed greens
10 cherry tomatoes

Preheat the oven to 350°F. Chop the kale, then place in a bowl and cover with boiling water. Leave for 5 minutes to soften. Drain and rinse under cold water.

While the kale is softening, trim the leek and finely slice. Crack the eggs into a bowl, add the oregano and season with salt and pepper. Whisk together with a fork.

Heat a frying pan with a splash of oil over medium heat. Add the leek and cook for 3–4 minutes until soft. Add the cooked kale and stir for a minute.

Wipe a large muffin tin with oil using a paper towel. Distribute the cooked kale and leek mix equally among the cups (6–8 of them), then pour the egg mix into the holes to fill them three-quarters full. Sprinkle the goat cheese on top along with the seeds and halved cherry tomatoes.

Place in the middle of the oven and bake for 10–15 minutes until each frittata is firm in the center. Using a spatula, loosen the sides gently, then flip out on to a wire rack to cool.

To pack: Place 3 or 4 frittatas on one side in each lunchbox with the mixed greens and cherry tomatoes alongside.

TRY THIS...

Swap the oregano and goat cheese for snipped fresh chives, crumbled feta and some smoked salmon.

Kale, chorizo, feta and onion jam frittata

3 cups chopped kale

3 oz. chorizo

1 red pepper

6 eggs

2 oz. feta

4 tablespoons ready-made onion jam (or make your own, *see opposite*)

2 tablespoons mixed seeds

½ cup mixed greens

Preheat the oven to 350°F.

Place the kale in a bowl, cover with boiling water and leave for 5 minutes. Drain and rinse under cold water, then squeeze out excess water.

Dice the chorizo. Remove the core and seeds from the red pepper. Dice half into small pieces and cut the other half into ½-inch-thick strips.

Crack the eggs into a bowl, add a pinch of salt and whisk together with a fork. Stir through the kale, diced red pepper, crumbled feta and onion jam.

Wipe a large muffin tin with oil using a paper towel. Pour the egg mix into the holes to fill them three-quarters full (you can make 6–8 frittatas). Sprinkle the seeds on top. Place in the middle of the oven and bake for 10–15 minutes until each frittata is firm in the center. Using a spatula, loosen the sides gently, then flip out on to a wire rack to cool.

To pack: Place 3 or 4 frittatas on one side in each lunchbox with the greens and red pepper strips alongside.

TRY THIS...

Make your own red onion chutney: sweat 4 finely sliced red onions in a splash of oil over low heat for 10 minutes until soft. Stir in 2 tablespoons sugar or honey and cook over medium heat, stirring regularly, until the onions are slightly caramelized.

SEEDED KALE + BUTTERMILK CHICKEN CAESAR SALAD

INGREDIENTS:

2 skinless boneless chicken breasts
olive oil
1 lemon
¼ cup mixed seeds (sesame, pumpkin
  and sunflower)
3 cups chopped kale
1 cucumber
¼ cup Parmesan shavings
2 portions of Buttermilk Caesar Dressing
  (see page 152)

TRY THIS…

· Swap the seeds for toasted mixed nuts.
  Crush them lightly before toasting to release
  more nutty flavour.

· Toast some chopped rye bread with crushed
  garlic and olive oil in the oven to create rye
  croutons. Pack these separately to sprinkle
  on the salad before eating.

METHOD:

Preheat the oven to 400°F. Place the chicken
breasts on a baking sheet and drizzle over a little
oil. Zest the lemon over the chicken and sprinkle
with half of the mixed seeds. Bake for 18–20
minutes until cooked through. Cool.

While the chicken is in the oven, place the kale
in a bowl, cover with boiling water and leave for
5 minutes to soften; drain and rinse under cold
water.

Slice the cucumber in half lengthways, and again
in half lengthways so you have 4 strips. Remove
the watery seeds with a small knife or teaspoon.
Dice the cucumber into ½-inch cubes. Toss with
the kale and Parmesan.

To pack: Spread the kale salad in the lunchboxes.
Slice the chicken at an angle into thin slices
and lay on top of the salad. Sprinkle over the
remaining seeds. Pack the dressing separately.

KALE + WALNUT PESTO SALAD

INGREDIENTS:

1 cup black quinoa
3 cups chopped kale
1½ cups frozen shelled edamame beans
2 tablespoons dried shredded coconut
2 portions of Kale and Walnut Pesto
  (see page 155)
4 tablespoons pomegranate seeds

TRY THIS…

Serve with a baked salmon fillet. Place 2 fillets, about 4 oz. each, on a lined baking sheet, sprinkle with a little oil and season with salt. Bake in a 400°F oven for 12 minutes. Leave to cool before flaking over the salad when packing.

METHOD:

Put the quinoa, 2 cups of water and a pinch of salt in a medium pot and bring to a boil. Reduce heat to low, cover and simmer 15–20 minutes until the liquid has been absorbed. Fluff with a fork. Tip into a bowl.

While the quinoa is cooking, roughly chop the kale, place in a bowl and cover with boiling water. Add a pinch of salt and leave for 5 minutes, then drain and rinse under cold water. Add to the bowl of quinoa.

Thaw the edamame in a bowl of cold water for 1–2 minutes, then drain.

Toast the coconut in a small dry pan over medium heat until golden. Add half to the quinoa bowl; keep the rest for garnish.

When making the pesto, add a little extra oil/water to create a loose consistency. Add the pesto to the quinoa bowl along with half of the pomegranate seeds and half the edamame beans. Toss all the ingredients together.

To pack: Spoon the salad into the lunchboxes. Sprinkle over the remaining toasted coconut, pomegranate seeds and edamame beans.

KALE RANCH SALAD

INGREDIENTS:

2 skinless boneless chicken breasts
olive oil for drizzling
4 tablespoons pumpkin seeds
2 strips of bacon
3 cups chopped kale
1 x 8.5-oz. can sweet corn kernels
1 tablespoon smoked paprika
2 handfuls of cherry tomatoes
2 portions of Buttermilk Caesar Dressing
   (see page 152), with extra Tabasco to taste

TRY THIS…

Use 2 corn on the cob instead of canned corn.
Place the corn cobs in a pan with about an inch
of water and add a pinch of salt. Simmer over a
medium heat for 6–7 minutes. Drain and rinse
under cold water. Once cool, shave the corn
kernels off the cob using a sharp knife.

METHOD:

Preheat the oven to 400°F. Place the chicken on a
baking sheet. Drizzle a little oil over the chicken
and sprinkle with half of the pumpkin seeds.
Lay the bacon on the tray alongside the chicken.
Bake the chicken for 18–20 minutes; remove the
bacon after 10–12 minutes, once golden. Cool.

While the chicken and bacon are in the oven,
place the kale in a bowl, cover with boiling water
and leave for 5 minutes to soften. Drain and
return to the bowl.

Drain the corn and place in a pan with a little
oil and the smoked paprika. Fry over high heat
for 3–5 minutes until some bits of corn are just
crisp. Cool.

Cut the cherry tomatoes in half and add to the
bowl of kale.

Slice the chicken at an angle into thin slices.
Gently break up the bacon with your fingers.

To pack: Spread the kale and cherry tomatoes
on the base of the lunchboxes. Top with the
fanned sliced chicken and sprinkle over the corn,
remaining pumpkin seeds and bacon. Pack the
dressing separately.

SAUCES
AND
DRESSINGS

BUTTERMILK CAESAR DRESSING

MAKES 4 LUNCHBOX PORTIONS

An alternative to a classic Caesar dressing, this works well on simple salads and alongside BBQ'd dishes and spicy dishes.

INGREDIENTS:

1 garlic clove
2 oz. Parmesan
2 tablespoons finely snipped fresh chives
1 cup buttermilk
4 drops of Tabasco
2 tablespoons Worcestershire sauce

METHOD:

Peel the garlic and crush into a bowl. Grate in the Parmesan. Add the remaining ingredients and whisk together with a fork. This can be kept in the fridge in an airtight container for 2–3 days.

TRY THIS...

· Make it your own by mixing the chives with other soft herbs or adding extra Tabasco, or crumbling through 2 oz. melted soft blue cheese.

· Swap the buttermilk for natural yogurt.

COCONUT-LIME DRESSING

A smooth coconut dressing with flavors that work especially well with Asian, fish and lentil-based dishes.

INGREDIENTS:

1 x 14-oz. can coconut milk
1–2 fresh green chili peppers
4 limes
4 tablespoons honey

METHOD:

Measure 1 cup of the creamy part of the coconut milk from the can. Pour this into a pan. Reserve the liquid part of the coconut milk in case you need to loosen the dressing at the end.

Finely dice the chili peppers (keeping or removing the seeds, depending on how much you like heat). Add to the pan.

Zest the limes into the pan and add the juice too. Bring to a boil, then immediately lower the heat and simmer for 10 minutes, stirring occasionally. The dressing will thicken into a syrupy consistency—stir in liquid coconut milk if the dressing becomes too thick.

Remove from the heat and stir in the honey. Season with salt and pepper. This can be kept in the fridge in an airtight container for 3–5 days. It also freezes well for 3 months in ice-cube trays. Thaw before using.

GREEN PESTO

MAKES 4 LUNCHBOX PORTIONS

Pestos are perfect for using up leftover herbs, greens and nuts. Pine nuts are traditional but unsalted cashews will create a similar, creamy pesto.

INGREDIENTS:

1 garlic clove (optional)
1–2 oz. Parmesan
40 fresh basil leaves
½ cup pine nuts (or other nuts)
3 tablespoons olive oil
juice of 1–2 lemons

METHOD:

Peel the garlic (if using). Turn on a food processor and drop the garlic on to the turning blades. Grate the Parmesan and add to the processor bowl along with the basil, pine nuts, oil and 3 tablespoons water. Blitz everything together for 2 minutes until broken down.

Add lemon juice to taste plus extra water, if needed, to reach your desired texture and flavor. The pesto should not be completely smooth but should run off the spoon like a thick sauce rather than a dip. Season well.

This can be kept in the fridge in an airtight container, covered with a thin layer of olive oil, for up to a week. It also freezes well for 3 months —place in ice-cube trays for individual portions and thaw before using.

TRY THIS...

· You can omit the Parmesan and use a splash of natural yogurt/almond milk for creaminess instead.

· Toasting the nuts will give a deeper color and flavor.

· Swap the basil for other soft herbs such as parsley/cilantro or use a mixture.

· Add a handful of arugula for pepperiness or spinach for a rich green flavor.

· Throw in a handful of seeds.

· Experiment with different cheeses—pecorino and Manchego both work well.

· Serve leftover pesto on toast topped with an egg at breakfast, or with crackers or raw slices of zucchini as a snack/starter.

2 MORE PESTO IDEAS

Red pepper pesto

Make the Green Pesto (*see opposite*), but add 1 jarred roasted red pepper and 5 sun-dried tomatoes and omit the water and oil when blitzing.

TRY THIS…

· Swap the Parmesan for feta.

· Add ½ fresh red chili pepper or a pinch of crushed red pepper for more heat.

Kale and walnut pesto

Soak ½ cup chopped kale in boiled water for 5 minutes, then drain and rinse in cold water. Make the Green Pesto (*see opposite*), but use walnuts instead of pine nuts and add the kale when blitzing.

THAI GREEN PASTE

MAKES 4 LUNCHBOX PORTIONS

This is a powerful, fresh green Thai sauce, great as a base for curries but also soups, or to add to stir-fries or melt into a dressing (it is solid because of the coconut oil, so melt in the microwave).

INGREDIENTS:

3 fresh green chilies
1 small piece fresh ginger
2 garlic cloves
1 small onion
½ cup fresh cilantro
1 teaspoon fish sauce
2 tablespoons coconut oil
1 lemongrass stick, tough outer parts removed
1 teaspoon black pepper
1 teaspoon ground cumin
1 tablespoon ground coriander
1 lime

METHOD:

Remove the core from the chilies (and the seeds too if you prefer). Peel the ginger and garlic. Peel and roughly chop the onion. Place all these prepared ingredients in a blender and add the cilantro, fish sauce, coconut oil, lemongrass and spices. Zest the lime into the blender and add the juice too. Blend until smooth.

Add a splash of water to loosen the paste to a thick sauce consistency. Season with a pinch of salt.

This can be kept in the fridge in an airtight container for 3–5 days. It also freezes well for 3 months (store in ice-cube trays so you can take a portion out as you need it); thaw before using.

SATAY DRESSING

MAKES 4 LUNCHBOX PORTIONS	METHOD:

This recipe works as a dip, sauce or loose dressing. The consistency can be adjusted simply by adding extra water. Great on salads or with stir-fries, it also can be used as a marinade for baked fish and meat.

INGREDIENTS:

1 small piece fresh ginger
1/3 cup peanut butter (preferably smooth and sugar-free)
8 teaspoons soy sauce
1/4 cup cilantro
2 teaspoons honey (optional)
1 fresh red chili pepper (optional)
zest and juice of 1–2 limes (optional)

Peel the ginger and drop into a blender. Add the peanut butter, soy sauce and cilantro and blend until smooth. Run the machine while adding hot water in small amounts to achieve a creamy consistency.

For a sweeter sauce, add the honey. If you want a kick of heat, add the chili pepper. Add the lime for zing.

This can be kept in the fridge in an airtight container for 3–5 days. It also freezes well for 3 months in ice-cube trays. Thaw before using.

PEANUT TERIYAKI SAUCE

MAKES 4 LUNCHBOX PORTIONS	METHOD:

A quick, homemade version of Japanese teriyaki, this includes nuts and sesame oil for a deeper flavor.

INGREDIENTS:

20 drops of Tabasco
4 teaspoons honey
4 teaspoons toasted sesame oil
1/4 cup soy sauce
1 tablespoon peanut butter (preferably smooth and sugar-free)

Combine all the ingredients in a small pan and simmer for 3 minutes over high heat. Keep stirring. Allow to cool.

This can be kept in the fridge in an airtight container for 3–5 days. It also freezes well for 3 months in ice-cube trays. Thaw before using.

HUMMUS

MAKES 4 LUNCHBOX PORTIONS	TRY THIS…
A dollop of hummus is a nice addition to any salad and another way of using up fresh and canned ingredients.	· For a classic hummus, add 1 teaspoon tahini, a pinch of ground cumin and ½ garlic clove when blitzing.
	· A handful of spinach/arugula blitzed in will give a green hummus.
INGREDIENTS:	· Stir in 3–4 tablespoons natural yogurt to make the hummus creamier (good with spicy food or eggs at breakfast).
1 x 15.5-oz. can chickpeas juice of 1 lemon 2 tablespoons olive oil	· Give the hummus a Middle Eastern twist with 2 teaspoons harissa paste.
METHOD:	· Blitz in the flesh from 1 avocado and a handful of fresh cilantro.
Drain and rinse the chickpeas, then tip into a food processor and add the lemon, oil and 1 tablespoon water. Blitz until smooth. If needed, add extra water to loosen to the desired consistency. Season to taste.	· Add 5 sun-dried tomatoes and a handful of fresh basil leaves when blitzing.
	· For a hot Mexican-style hummus, add a handful of jarred jalapeños and fresh lime juice when blitzing.
This can be kept in the fridge in an airtight container for 3–5 days.	· Finish with a tablespoon of any of our pestos (*see pages 154–155*).

2 MORE HUMMUS IDEAS

Beetroot hummus	*Red pepper and butter bean hummus*
1 x 15.5-oz. can chickpeas, drained and rinsed juice of 1 lemon 3 cooked and peeled beets 2 tablespoons olive oil 1 tablespoon water	1 x 15.5-oz. can butter beans juice of 1 lemon 1 jarred roasted red pepper (4 pieces) 2 tablespoons olive oil 1 tablespoon water
Follow the method for Hummus (above).	Follow the method for Hummus (above).

INDEX

Da Capo Press
Hachette Book Group
1290 Avenue of the Americas, New York, NY 10104
www.dacapopress.com
@dacapopress

Printed in the United States of America

Originally published in 2017 by Ebury Press, an
imprint of Ebury Publishing, in the UK.

First U.S. Edition: May 2018

Published by Da Capo Press, an imprint of
Perseus Books, LLC, a subsidiary of Hachette
Book Group, Inc. The Da Capo Press name and logo
is a trademark of the Hachette Book Group.

The publisher is not responsible for websites (or
their content) that are not owned by the publisher.

Photography © Naomi Twigden and Anna Pinder,
except for pages 15, 31, 75, 105 © Charlie Taylor 2017

Print book interior design by Louise Evans

Library of Congress Control Number: 2017956460

ISBNs: 978-0-7382-3487-8 (paperback),
978-0-7382-3486-1 (e-book)

LSC-C

10 9 8 7 6 5 4 3 2 1

ACKNOWLEDGEMENTS

We'd like to thank everyone who has helped
us at Lunch BXD and on this book. Our parents
Rebecca & Ivan and Kate & Mark, David (thank
you for your on going patience, support and
guidance), Rach (you are a constant inspiration
to me, thank you for your never-failing support,
love, encouragement and for donning chef
whites in times of need! –*Anna*), Kate (we never
would have begun this adventure without you),
Freya and Courtney (our dream team), Moira,
Fred, Hannah Struve (for lending us her beautiful
ceramics), Celia, Kerry, Jess, Laura, Barney and
everyone who ordered one of our lunchboxes
and supported our Lunch BXD adventure.